THE BOOK OF

Chinese
COOKING

THE BOOK OF

Chinese

COOKING

JASPER SPENCER-SMITH

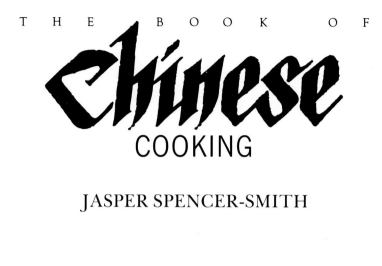

Photography by
RAYMOND BRAGG

HPBooks

ANOTHER BEST-SELLING VOLUME FROM HPBOOKS

HPBOOKS
Published by The Berkley Publishing Group
200 Madison Avenue
New York, NY 10016

10 9 8 7 6 5

By arrangement with Salamander Books Ltd.

Notice: The information contained in this book is true and complete
to the best of our knowledge. All recommendations are made without
any guarantees on the part of the author or the publisher. The author
and publisher disclaim all liability in connection with the use of this
information.

   Library of Congress Cataloging-in-Publication Data
Spencer-Smith, Jasper
   The book of Chinese cooking / Jasper Spencer-Smith.
      p.   cm.
   Includes index.
   ISBN 1 - 55788 - 033 - 6
   1. Cookery, Chinese.   I. Title.
TX724.5.C5S639 1991
641.5951- dc20
                                              91-13565
                                                  CIP

This book was created by Pegasus Editions Limited,
Premier House, Hinton Road, Bournemouth, Dorset BH1 2EF
Printed and bound in Spain by Bookprint, S.L.

CONTENTS

INTRODUCTION

The testimony to the inherent quality and appeal of Chinese cooking is the way it has captured the imagination and respect of cooks, top chefs and food-lovers throughout the West. This is hardly surprising since it is one of the richest, many-faceted and purest in the world.

The unique style of sophisticated simplicity has been developed over centuries through the expertise of one of the world's oldest, most advanced civilization.

The vast, varied landmass and long coastline of China provide a wealth of diverse, natural foods, which Chinese cooks, with their deep reverence for the 'fruits' of nature, have cleverly and carefully transformed into a variety of styles. These span the whole spectrum, from the subtle delicacy of steamed dim sum to the fiery piquancy of Szechuan Hot & Sour Soup.

Chinese cooks have drawn on their culinary knowledge to create the most suitable, delicious, yet economical uses for every food, and they have discovered the best ways of combining foods to emphasize to perfection textures, tastes, colors and aromas. Rich foods are counterbalanced by bland ones, brightly colored ingredients are juxtaposed with pale, smooth textures contrasted by crunch, and a hot dish by a cold one.

Despite its 5,000 year-old roots, Chinese cooking is up-to-date. It is fresh, light, practical and relevant to today's lifestyles and needs.

The Chinese do not believe in complicated dishes, preferring to allow the food to speak for itself. Cooking equipment is simple, kept to a minimum, and makes efficient use of heat.

Through authentic recipes, THE BOOK OF CHINESE COOKING captures the essential, living spirit of true Chinese food, and enables you to take advantage, today, of centuries of experience to recreate with ease, in your own kitchen masterly, harmonious dishes.

REGIONAL CHINESE COOKING

China is a vast country extending from the sub-tropical regions of Hunan and Kwantung in the south right up to the dry plains of Mongolia in the north, while the western borders go right into central Asia, reaching almost to the frontier of Afghanistan. Being so large there are dramatic contrasts in geography and climate across the country. The great diversity of regional history, customs, life and culture have caused a distinct cuisine to evolve in each of the four major provinces.

NORTH

The cooking of Peking and northern China is a fusion of three distinct influences, high-class court and mandarin dishes, rustic Mongolian and Manchurian fare, and the indigenous cooking of the cold, northerly climate. Consequently, variations in the refinement, elegance and lightness of the foods can be noticed.

Throughout the area, though, rice has taken a back seat to wheat. This is immediately apparent in the number and variety of pancakes, noodles, dumplings, breads and buns that are to be found everywhere. Stir-frying is less common, but barbecueing, laqueur roasting, spit-roasting, slow-simmering and deep-frying are popular.

Sauces are richly flavored with dark soy sauce, garlic, green onions and spices; and sesame oil is used more frequently than elsewhere.

Lamb, a meat largely disliked elsewhere in China, is eaten in northern areas due to the Mongolian influence.

WEST

The Szechuan cuisine tends to be hearty rather than delicate, and is renowned for highly spiced foods, especially dishes containing chiles. Szechuan cooks have also perfected a fascinating range of hot-sour, savory-spiced and sweet-hot-piquant recipes. Many are characterized by the crunch and bite of pickles, for in this inland region the preservation of foods by pickling in salt and vinegar is popular, as is smoking.

Unlike many dishes in eastern China, in the west a number of dishes are fried with only enough sauce to convey seasonings, and so the sauce itself is not an important element of the dish. As a result, dishes are drier and more reminiscent of southern stir-fries.

Multiple flavors are another feature in the cuisine of the west, and it is quite usual to find garlic, chiles, vinegar and soy sauce in one dish.

EAST

The cooking of the east is more starchy, and richer — not only in the amount of lard and oil used in cooking (although this is usually either left in the pan, or allowed to fall to the bottom of the bowl and not eaten), but also in the range of ingredients, the amount of soy sauce, and number and combinations of spices.

Another significant characteristic is the heavier use of rice. Not only is it served plain as an accompaniment, but is also combined with vegetables, and used as a stuffing. Rice-based products such as the widely used rice wine, exist in profusion. With a long coastline, and well-watered lands, a fine selection of seafood and plenty of freshwater fish are caught. A great range of vegetables is also available.

People of Shanghai are sweet-toothed and use sugar fairly liberally, making savory dishes that are generally sweeter than elsewhere.

SOUTH

To many people, the cooking of Canton is exemplified by stir-frying in a wok. But this is only part of the picture. Southern cooking is probably the most inventive, rich and colorful in China. It has been influenced by a steady stream of foreign traders and travellers, and is richly endowed with year-round produce from land and sea, thanks to the sub-tropical climate and longest coastline of the Chinese provinces.

Fruits flourish and are combined in meat and savory dishes more here than elsewhere. Vegetables are used in quantity, but meat sparsely. As well as stir-frying, steaming and roasting are prevalent and the use of oil in cooking kept to a minimum. Every meal includes rice, and exotic ingredients such as shark's fin and birds nests are common. Southern dishes are often sauced with thick but delicate sauces.

The area produces some of the best soy sauce in the country, and, because of this, specializes in 'red cooking', slowly baking or braising in soy sauce until the liquid has evaporated, to add an attractive red color to the food.

CHINESE MEALS

When composing a meal, as when composing a dish, Chinese always consider the contrasts between the flavors, colors, textures and aromas of all the dishes, and make sure they achieve a good balance. Chinese also distinguish between salty, sweet, sour, hot, bitter, bland, aromatic and cool. The dipping sauces and seasonings on a table can add a dramatic touch to the occasional mouthful.

The number of dishes served at a Chinese meal will depend on the number of diners; generally there is one course per diner. Dishes are not served in any particular order, but tend to arrive as they are cooked. Soups are not served at the start of a meal; instead, they come somewhere in the middle or even at the end as their function is to wash down the rice. In some meals there may be two soups, the first being served as a second course. As a general rule, an everyday Chinese meal will not finish with a sweet, although there may sometimes be fruit. However at the end of banquets or elaborate feasts there may be a dessert.

Dishes are communal, with everyone helping themselves to portions of everything.

As each dish must be within the reach of everyone, round tables are used, often with rotating centers, so no-one has to stretch to reach any dish.

Dim sum, which literally means 'little heart' or 'to dot the heart', are eaten only at lunchtime or as snacks at odd times of the day, even just before going to bed. Traditionally, they would not be eaten at a main meal, although their popularity in the West has caused many restaurants to flout tradition. Dim sum can be sweet or savory, they can be deep-fried, poached, baked or braised, but most often they are steamed dumplings with various fillings which come to the table in round wooden or bamboo containers piled one on top of each other. Dim sum may also be miniature versions of a main course dish, such as tiny spare ribs or baby pancake rolls.

INGREDIENTS

All of the ingredients used in THE BOOK OF CHINESE COOKING can be bought readily from Chinese food shops and special delicatessens. An increasing number, some of which may even be from a Western source, can also be found in good supermarkets. Those that are not are usually added as optional ingredients or alternatives suggested.

VEGETABLES

Bean sprouts – these small, young tender shoots are usually mung beans that have germinated, although other beans can also be allowed to sprout. Bean sprouts are nutritious, containing generous amounts of vitamins and minerals, and add a delicious crunch to stir-fry dishes.

Chinese beans – the tender pods of these green beans can be eaten whole. Snap beans or French beans can be substituted.

Chinese cabbage (bok choy) — the most widely available of Chinese green vegetables. The stalks have a mild, refreshing flavor, and the leaves are pleasantly tangy with a slight bitterness.

Chinese flowering cabbage (choy sum) — very similar to 'bok choy', though slightly smaller, with narrower stalks and slightly paler green leaves; the distinctive feature is the yellow flowers. These are cooked with the rest of the vegetables.

Celery cabbage (wong ah bok) — delicate pale green vegetable with a sweet taste that makes it ideal for use in salads. Its delicate flavor blends superbly with other foods.

Cilantro – cilantro resembles flat-leaved parsley in appearance, but it smells and tastes very different. Both of these are quite distinctive, and not immediately appealing to some people, but it does not take long for any initial reservations to be overcome and it can quickly become a firm favorite.

Fresh cilantro wilts quickly so buy as near as possible to the time of using; or grow your own.

Daikon – daikon is the Far Eastern variety of winter radish that is also called 'mooli'. Being long, white and fat it looks more like a giant carrot than the small, round, red radish that is commonly seen in the West. Daikon is eaten both raw in salads, and cooked in vegetable dishes. It is also pickled.

FRUIT

Lychees – canned lychees are a 'staple' dessert in many Chinese restaurants. But when making Chinese meals at home, look for fresh lychees as they are now becoming far more readily available. They need no more preparation than using the fingers to easily crack the nobbly, brittle coating. Beneath it, delicious, perfumed white flesh surrounds a smooth central seed. Neither the skin nor the seed are eaten.

Mango – there are many different types of mango, each one varying in size, shape and color. But whichever is available, select fruit that feels heavy for its size and is free of bruises or damage. A ripe mango yields to gentle pressure and should have an enticing, scented aroma. The flesh inside should have a wonderful, luxurious and slightly exotic texture and flavor, but poor quality fruit can be disappointing; the key is the fragrance.

If a mango is a little firm when bought, leave it in a warm sunny place to finish ripening.

Star fruit – star-fruit are long, almost translucent yellow, ridged fruit; they are also known as 'carambola'. The whole fruit is edible, and when cut across the width, the slices resemble five-pointed stars. Raw star-fruit have a pleasant, citrus-like, juicy sharpness, but when poached lightly the flavor is more distinctive.

CORNSTARCH MIXTURE

Measure spoons of cornstarch into a bowl, then stir in twice the amount of water. Pour into a screw-top jar and keep in the refrigerator. Stir or shake jar before measuring out required amount.

INGREDIENTS

Black beans, salted fermented — these very salty soy beans are available in cans and plastic packages.

Chinese five-spice powder — a warmly aromatic blend of spices.

ChingKiang vinegar — the most well-known brand of Chinese black vinegar. Black vinegars are made from grains other than rice, and aged to impart complex, smoky flavors with a light, pleasant bitterness. Substitute sherry, balsamic vinegar or a good red wine vinegar.

Gingko nuts — these have a hard shell, which must be removed before cooking, and a creamy-colored flesh. Shelled gingko nuts are also available in cans. If unavailable, substitute almonds.

Hoisin sauce — a reddish-brown sauce based on soy beans, and flavored with garlic, chiles and a combination of spices. Flavors vary between brands, but it is nearly always quite sweet and it can range from the thickness of a soft jam to a runny sauce.

Mushrooms — Chinese cooks seldom buy fresh mushrooms, preferring to use dried ones. These must be soaked before cooking — put the mushrooms into a bowl, cover with boiling water, cover the bowl, leave for about 20 to 30 minutes until swollen and pliable, then drain well. If the stems are tough, discard them. *Winter black mushrooms* — with a fairly intense, fragrant flavor, these are the most widely used.

Cloud ear — also known as 'wood ear', these are added for their texture rather than flavor, as they have little.

Straw — these thin, tall, leaflike mushrooms are also known as 'paddy straw' or 'grass' mushrooms. They are canned as well as dried.

Oyster sauce — made from oysters, salt, seasonings and nowadays, cornstarch and coloring.

Pickled and preserved vegetables — various types of vegetables, preserved, or pickled, in salt, are available in cans and plastic pouches, but if a label simply specifies *'Preserved Vegetable'*, it will invariably mean mustard greens.

Turnip — these are not Western turnips, but a type of radish.

Rice vinegar — the mildest of all vinegars, with a sweet, delicate flavor and comes in several varieties. If possible, use a pale rice vinegar for light colored sweet-and-sour dishes, and try a dark variety for dipping sauces. If unable to find either, use cider vinegar.

Rice wine — similar to sherry in color, bouquet and alcohol content (18%), but with its own distinctive flavor. Shaoshin is the most famous brand. Substitute a good dry sherry if unavailable.

Rose Wine — imparts an exotic quality to foods. Use sweet sherry as a substitute.

Soy sauce — made from fermented soy beans, a good soy sauce has a rich aroma and a salty, pungent flavor that heightens other flavors. Many qualities and grades are available. Many mass-produced ones are chemically fermented hydrolized protein, but they can easily be detected. A thick, foamy head that takes quite a while to disperse will form on the top of naturally fermented soy sauce when the bottle is shaken vigorously, whereas the bubbles on top of a chemically-fermented product fade quickly. Dark soy is used with dark meats and dipping sauces; light soy with vegetables, seafood and soups.

Sesame oil — this is made from toasted sesame seeds. The thicker and browner the oil, the more aromatic it is. Sesame oil enlivens other flavors. Care is needed when cooking with sesame oil as it tends to burn easily; Chinese cooks usually sprinkle a few drops over a dish immediately before removing from the heat.

Shrimp paste — concentrated, salty and with a pronounced shrimp-like flavor and smell.

Star anise — a dark brown, dried 8-pointed star-shaped spice. It has a distinctive aniseed flavor, with liquorice overtones.

Szechuan peppercorns — reddish colored, with a mildly hot flavor, and a spicy fragrance reminiscent of coriander seeds. Buy whole seeds if possible as the flavor deteriorates more quickly when ground.

Yellow bean paste — made from fermented soy beans, it is salty and pungent and may be chunky or smooth.

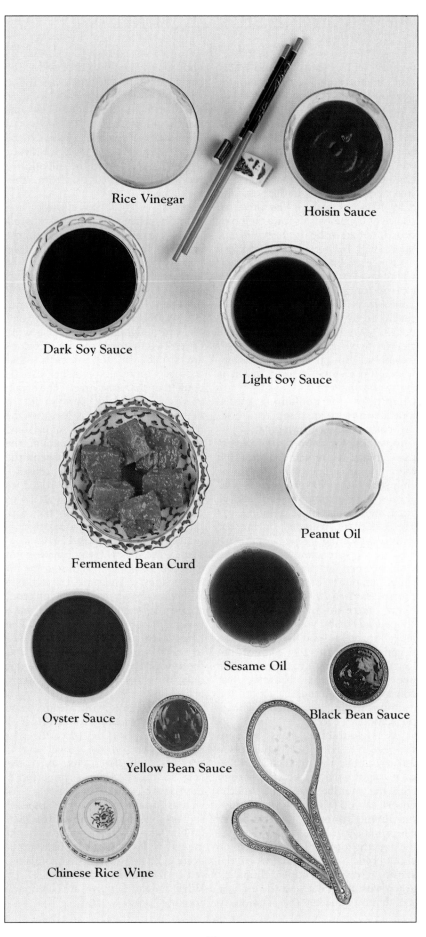

Rice Vinegar

Hoisin Sauce

Dark Soy Sauce

Light Soy Sauce

Fermented Bean Curd

Peanut Oil

Sesame Oil

Oyster Sauce

Black Bean Sauce

Yellow Bean Sauce

Chinese Rice Wine

CHINESE EQUIPMENT

Chinese cooks often spend more time in the kitchen preparing the ingredients than in cooking them. Cooking utensils are few, practical and versatile, and are designed to make the most efficient and economical use of heat.

Chopping board – a planed slice of tree, about 15-inches in diameter and 8 to 10-inches high, is the preferred choice of Chinese chefs for a chopping board, but an ordinary, heavy plastic board will be perfectly satisfactory for domestic kitchens in the West.

Cleaver – Chinese cooks use a cleaver for all tasks that require a knife, from carving delicate flower shapes from vegetables to chopping bones. A Chinese chef selects the cleaver that has the right size and weight for his physique. Frequent honing on a stone ensures that it is always razor-sharp.

Chopsticks, for cooking – special long chopsticks are used for cooking, particularly stir-frying.

Chopsticks, for eating – the important points to remember are that there is an upper and a lower chopstick, the lower one should always be held stationary, the square ends should be held pointing upwards and the rounded or tapered ends downwards.

Pick up the chopsticks as you would a pen or pencil and let an equal amount of the chopstick protrude on each side of the hand. Now, instead of holding the chopsticks with your thumb and index finger, as you would hold a pencil, hold with the tips of the fourth or the little finger and let the upper part of the chopstick rest comfortably in the base of the thumb and the index finger. This is the stationary chopstick.

With your other hand, pick up the second chopstick and place directly above the first, and parallel to it. Hold the upper stick firmly with the thumb, index and middle fingers as you would a pencil. Use the thumb to brace the stationary chopstick securely against the tip of the fourth finger. There should be about 1-inch of space between the sticks. Press the upper chopstick down with the index and third finger so that it meets the stationary

chopstick to pick up the food. Tap the ends of the chopsticks gently on the table to make sure they are even as chopsticks will not work efficiently unless aligned.

Skimmer – shallow, wide, metal mesh skimmers are used for lifting deep-fried food from the oil, and for serving pieces of food from 'pot-style' meals.

Spatula – for efficiency, safety and comfort when stir-frying a spatula with a curved blade that follows the contours of the wok, and a long handle that allows the hand to be kept well away from the heat, is used.

Steamers – Chinese cooks use bamboo steamers, that have no bottom, and are designed to sit over a wok. Often two or more steaming baskets are stacked on top of each other so that a number of dishes can be cooked at the same time. The steam is absorbed by the bamboo lid so that water does not drip onto the food. So that all the nourishing juices and flavor are retained, the food is often placed on a plate in the steamer and served directly from it.

Whisk – a whisk about 10-inches long and consisting of thin strips of bamboo tied together at the top, rather like a witches broomstick, is used for cleaning a wok.

Wok – the wok is the cornerstone of Chinese cooking. Woks come in many sizes. They are curved like a shallow bowl, are made of iron, copper or stainless steel, and have two handles on opposite sides. The flared sides permit easy, rapid tossing of a number of ingredients and the use of the minimum of oil, not only for stir-frying but also deep-frying.

To hold the wok steady it is placed on a metal, perforated ring. If you have a gas stove, place the ring right-side up on the stove, but if you cook by electricity, turn the ring so the bottom is uppermost. Electric woks are also available. As well as for stir-frying, woks are used for deep-frying, braising, steaming, boiling, crystal-boiling and red cooking. A wok is often supplied with a domed lid for using when braising, red cooking and crystal boiling.

Wire ladels – these are used for cooking Potato Nests, page 103.

WESTERN EQUIPMENT

While it may make a cook feel that they are being truly authentic if they use Chinese utensils, it is not necessary to buy any special equipment. The equipment that is available in the average Western home kitchen is quite adequate for the preparation and cooking of a whole range of Chinese dishes.

Chopping board – a conventional, heavy plastic chopping board can be used quite satisfactorily.

Food processor – a food processor with a selection of slicing discs is very useful for quickly, neatly and evenly slicing and chopping for stir-frying.

Kitchen knives – a selection of sharp, strong-bladed knives will help with the quick, efficient cutting and slicing of ingredients.

Skillets– ordinary skillets can be used in place of a wok. A light-weight skillet is preferable for stir-frying as it will heat up quickly and convey the intense heat that is required. The most practical pans are those that are wide and have deep sides, as they allow the food to be tossed and stirred more easily. They will also prevent the various ingredients from being too close together, which slows down the cooking and can hamper the food becoming crisp.

Slotted spoon – can be as effective as a wire skimmer for removing food from deep oil or cooking liquids.

Steamer – a Western-style steamer can be used in place of a bamboo steamer, but it is a good idea to line the lid with paper towels to prevent drips of water falling onto the food.

Tongs – tongs can be used for turning and lifting food, instead of cooking chopsticks.

COOKING TECHNIQUES

Stir-frying – the essentials for good stir-frying are very little oil, food that is finely sliced or shredded with every piece cut to the same size, the use of a high heat so the food is cooked quickly, and tossing the ingredients.

The wok is put over a high heat, a little oil is poured and when really hot, the flavoring vegetables, such as garlic and gingerroot, are added. After a few seconds stirring, the meat goes into the wok, is stirred and tossed for a minute or two then removed. Next come the vegetables in the order of the length of cooking they require. When they have all been stirred and tossed for the requisite time, the meat is returned to the wok, and seasonings added. The food must then be served immediately to preserve its crispness.

Deep frying – Chinese deep-frying is done in a wok, so uses less oil. Foods are often marinated first in soy sauce and spices, and sometimes are coated in batter; a mixture of cornstarch and egg white is the most usual. Often, the food is fried until almost cooked, then removed from the oil, the oil reheated and the food added again to finish cooking and become really crisp.

Steaming – steaming is far more popular in China than in the West and is used to cook meat, poultry, fish, dim sum, other pastries and desserts. It was developed as a fuel saving measure as several foods can be cooked at once in baskets, which in China are made of bamboo, stacked above each other. Foods that require the most cooking are put to cook first, and those needing less time are placed on top in succession, as the cooking proceeds.

Red cooking – food, usually in large pieces, is cooked slowly in dark soy sauce, sometimes with other flavorings added. During the lengthy cooking, which may be as long as 4 hours, the soy imparts a fairly dark, reddish brown color and a rich flavor to the food. Because of the large amount of soy sauce that is used, the food can also be salty, so sugar may be added to counteract it.

Roasting – few domestic kitchens in China have an oven so roast Chinese dishes are usually those that are made in restaurants or the homes of well-to-do families.

—— VEGETABLE CUTTING ——

ROLL CUTTING

Cut a diagonal slice from the vegetable. Make a one-quarter turn of the vegetable towards you and make a diagonal slice slightly above and partly across the face of the first slice. Continue until vegetable is completely cut.

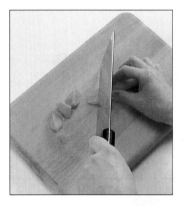

DIAGONAL CUTTING

Using a Chinese cleaver, or sharp heavy-bladed chef knife, hold the knife at a 45 degree angle to the surface of the food, and slice across diagonally, at a 45 degree angle. Move the knife along the length of the width of slice desired; make another cut, and continue along the length of the food.

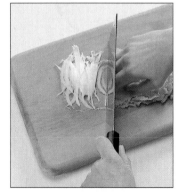

SHREDDING

Cut the sides and ends of the vegetables so that they are flat. Hold the vegetables firmly with the fingertips. Work the knife across the vegetables, moving the blade up and down and just in front of the fingers, moving the fingers along the vegetable closely followed by the knife. Cut the vegetable lengthwise across the slices to the width of a matchstick.

PREPARING SHRIMP

In China, shrimp that are larger than the shrimp most commonly seen in the West are used. Jumbo shrimp are the best type to use when making Chinese recipes. The dark vein that runs down the back of the shrimp must always be removed before the shrimp is cooked.

Break off or cut off the head if present, then slip off the body shell and remove the legs; the tail section may be left on. (The heads and shells can be reserved for cooking).

Run the point of a sharp knife lightly down its back and carefully pull away the dark vein; discard.

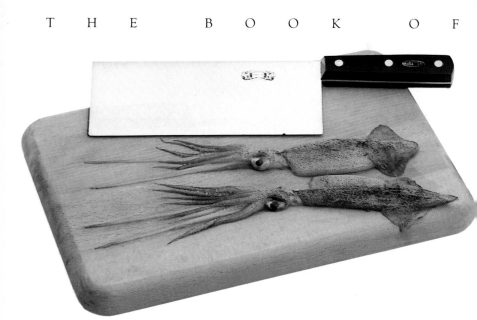

PREPARING SQUID

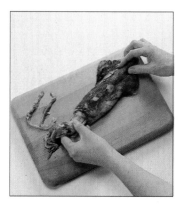

Squid are very popular in China and are sold fresh and frozen (squid freeze well) in all Chinese fish markets.

Plump, large squid are preferred for their flavor, texture and the decorative appearance they can add to a dish. The tentacles are cut across their width so the slices resemble stars; they are then used in stir-fry dishes, tossed in salads or coated in batter and deep-fried.

Thoroughly rinse the squid. Holding the head just below the eyes, gently pull it away from the body pouch, bringing the ink sac and other soft viscera with it. Discard the body pouch, but reserve the ink sac if desired.

Ease back the edge of the body pouch to locate the fine, stiff 'pen', then pull it out and discard.

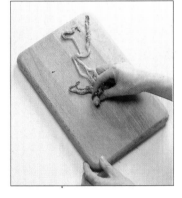

Cut the tentacles from the head just below the eyes; discard the head. Cut away the cartilage at the base of the tentacles. Squeeze off the beak-like mouth in the center of the mass of tentacles.

Peel off the skin of the body pouch, then cut away the edible fins. Rinse the squid, then cut across the body into slices.

——— SPRING ROLL SKINS ———

3/4 cup all-purpose flour
1/2 cup cornstarch
3 tablespoons vegetable oil
About 1-3/4 cups water

In a bowl, stir together flour, cornstarch, oil and enough water to make a thin batter.

Heat a lightly oiled, 6-inch skillet, spoon 2 tablespoons batter into center of pan and swirl it quickly around to cover bottom of pan.

Cook until the crepe is dry but not colored and the edges shrink from the sides of the pan.

Transfer to a plate, cover with a damp cloth. Repeat until all the batter has been used.

Makes 20 spring roll skins

To fill the skins, lay one out flat on a work surface. Place a portion of filling slightly off-center.

Fold the sides of the skin neatly over the filling, then roll-up to enclose the filling completely. Brush around the edges with beaten egg to seal.

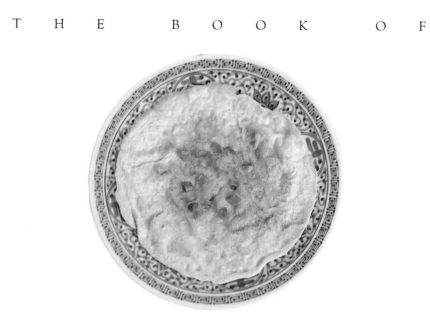

CHINESE OMELET

In a bowl, lightly beat together the two eggs. Heat a dry, preferably non-stick, small skillet.

Pour in the eggs, stir lightly while tipping the pan so the raw egg flows onto the dry area.

Cook for about 2 minutes until the underside is set and the top still slightly liquid. Turn the omelet over and cook the other side for about 2 minutes, until set.

TEA EGGS

8 eggs
3 tablespoons Keemun black tea
1 tablespoon sea salt
1 teaspoon Chinese five-spice powder
2 tablespoons dark soy sauce

Simmer eggs, just covered by water 8 to 10 minutes. Cool under cold running water 5 minutes. Roll and tap the eggs gently to crack their shells, but do not detach the shells from the eggs.

In a saucepan just large enough to hold the eggs in a single layer, mix tea, salt, five-spice powder and soy sauce with enough water to cover the eggs; bring to a boil.

Place eggs in pan and simmer 30 minutes. Turn off the heat and let eggs cool completely in the mixture. Peel off the shells to serve.

Makes 4 servings.

PORK DIM SUM

3/4 pound ground pork
1/4 pound raw shelled shrimp, ground
1-1/2 tablespoons soy sauce
1/2 tablespoon Chinese rice wine or dry sherry
1/2 tablespoon sesame oil
1/2 tablespoon sugar
Dash of pepper
1 egg white
1-1/2 tablespoons cornstarch
30 won-ton skins
Fresh or frozen green peas or chopped
    hard-cooked egg yolks, for garnish

To make filling: Mix together ground pork, ground shrimp, soy sauce, rice wine or sherry, sesame oil, sugar, pepper and egg white until mixture is well blended and smooth. Stir in cornstarch. Divide into 30 portions. Cut off the edges of won-ton skins to form circles, if necessary. Place 1 portion of filling in the middle of a won-ton skin. Gather the edges of the won-ton skin around the meat filling. Dip a teaspoon in water and use to smooth the surface of the meat.

Garnish by placing a green pea or chopped egg yolk on top of meat. Gather the edges to form a waist. Repeat with remaining won-ton skins and meat filling. Line a steamer with a damp cloth; steam over high heat 5 minutes. Remove and serve.

Makes 30 dumplings.

SHRIMP DIM SUM

3/4 pound raw shelled shrimp, ground
1 (4-oz.) can bamboo shoots, chopped
4 tablespoons water
1-1/2 tablespoons soy sauce
1/2 tablespoon Chinese rice wine or dry sherry
1/2 teaspoon sugar
1/2 teaspoon sesame oil
Dash of pepper
1-1/2 tablespoons cornstarch

Dough:
2-1/2 cups all-purpose flour
2/3 cup boiling water
1/3 cup cold water
1 tablespoon vegetable oil

To make filling: Mix together all ingredients except cornstarch until the mixture is well blended and smooth. Stir in cornstarch. Divide into 30 portions.

To make dough: Put 2 cups of the flour in a medium size bowl. Reserve remaining flour and use for hands if they become sticky. Stir in the boiling water. Add the cold water and oil. Mix to form dough; knead until smooth. Roll the dough into a long, rope shape and cut it into 30 pieces. Use a rolling pin to roll each portion into a thin 2-inch circle.

Place 1 portion of the filling in the middle of a dough circle. Bring the opposite edges together and pinch them together to hold. Repeat with remaining circles and filling.

Line a steamer with a damp cloth. Set the dumplings about 1 inch apart. Steam over high heat 5 minutes. Remove and serve.

Makes 30 dumplings.

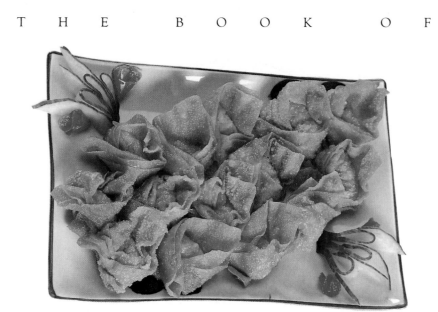

FRIED WON TONS

6 ounces ground pork
1/2 (4-oz.) can water chestnuts, finely chopped
1 tablespoon water
1 tablespoon cornstarch
1/2 teaspoon salt
1/2 teaspoon Chinese rice wine or dry sherry
Dash of sesame oil
Dash of pepper
30 won-ton skins
Vegetable oil for frying

To make filling: Mix together all ingredients except won-ton skins and vegetable oil until meat and water chestnuts are combined into a uniform mixture. Divide into 30 portions.

Put 1 tablespoon of the filling in the middle of a won-ton skin. Diagonally fold the skin in half to form a triangle. Fold the edge containing the filling over about 1/2 inch. Bring the 2 points together, moisten one inner edge and pinch the edges together to hold. Repeat with remaining won tons and filling.

Heat a wok, then add the vegetable oil. Deep fry the won tons over a medium heat until golden. Drain on paper towels and serve.

Makes 30 won tons.

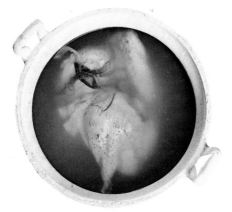

— CHINESE CHICKEN STOCK —

1/2 stewing chicken
1 ham hock, split
4 slices root gingerroot
4 green onions, chopped
1 tablespoon chopped parsley
2 quarts water

Place all ingredients in a large saucepan and bring to a boil. Skim. Reduce heat so liquid simmers, cover and cook 3 hours.

Pour into a sieve lined with cheesecloth, placed over a large bowl. Cool completely in a bowl of iced water or refrigerator. Store, covered, in the refrigerator, or freeze in convenient quantities.

Makes 7 cups.

Note: Chinese cooks use Chicken Stock for fish dishes (they do not make fish stock). If fish stock is preferred, substitute a favorite recipe.

- CHINESE VEGETABLE STOCK -

2 tablespoons vegetable oil
1 slice gingerroot, peeled
2-3/4 cups bean sprouts
3/4 cup sliced carrots
2 ounces dried straw mushrooms, soaked in hot
    water 20 minutes, drained
2 ounces dried black winter mushrooms, soaked
    in hot water 25 minutes
1 teaspoon rice wine or dry sherry
8 cups water
2 teaspoons sea salt

In a large saucepan, heat oil, add ginger-root and fry 2 minutes. Add bean sprouts and stir-fry 2 minutes.

Stir in remaining ingredients, bring to a boil, reduce heat so liquid simmers, cover and cook 45 minutes. Pour through a sieve lined with cheesecloth, placed over a large bowl. Cool completely, skim oil from surface and store in the refrigerator up to 3 days, or freeze in convenient quantities.

Makes 8 cups.

——— MUSHROOM SOUP ———

24 dried black winter mushrooms, soaked in hot
    water 25 minutes, drained
1/2-inch piece gingerroot, peeled and cut into 6
    slices
2 green onions, finely chopped
6 cups Chinese Chicken Stock, page 29
2 teaspoons rice wine or dry sherry
1-1/2 teaspoons sea salt
1 teaspoon brown sugar
Parsley, to garnish

Trim mushrooms and place in a small
saucepan with half the gingerroot and half
the green onions. Add 1/2 teaspoon salt
and cover with cold water. Bring slowly
to a boil, then simmer 3 minutes.

Drain. Pour stock into a medium
saucepan, add mushroom mixture and
remaining ingredients. Bring slowly to a
boil, reduce heat, cover, and simmer
gently 30 to 35 minutes. Serve hot
garnished with parsley.

Makes 4 servings.

— LAMB & CUCUMBER SOUP —

1 tablespoon dark soy sauce
1 teaspoon sesame oil
8 ounces lean lamb, cut into strips
6 cups Chinese Chicken Stock, page 29
1/2 teaspoon sea salt
White pepper
1 large cucumber, cut into paper thin slices
1 tablespoon rice vinegar

In a bowl, mix together soy sauce and sesame oil. Stir in lamb to coat and let stand 30 minutes. Bring chicken stock to boil; season with salt and pepper. Reduce heat so stock just simmers.

Lift lamb from bowl, add to stock and poach 2 minutes. Remove lamb and keep warm. Add cucumber to pan and return to a boil. Reduce heat so stock simmers, add lamb and vinegar and cook 4 minutes.

Makes 4 servings.

CHICKEN & ASPARAGUS SOUP

2 cups Chinese Chicken Stock, page 29
12 button mushrooms, sliced
2 tablespoons Cornstarch Mixture, page 10
1-1/2 cups finely sliced, cooked chicken breast
1/2 cup chopped asparagus tips, drained
3/4 cup cooked or canned whole-kernel corn,
    drained
1-1/2 teaspoons sea salt
1 teaspoon sesame oil, to serve
2 green onions, finely chopped, to garnish

In a saucepan bring chicken stock to a
boil.   Add the mushrooms, simmer 2
to 3 minutes, then stir in Cornstarch
Mixture and simmer, still stirring until
thickened.   Reduce heat, add chicken,
asparagus and corn and heat through
gently but thoroughly. Season with salt.

Serve sprinkled with sesame oil and garnished with chopped green onions.

Makes 4 servings.

—— HOT & SOUR SOUP ——

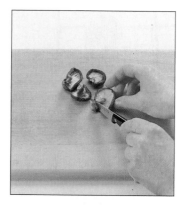

4 dried black winter mushrooms, soaked in hot
  water 25 minutes
1/4 (14-oz.) can Szechuan preserved vegetables,
  finely sliced
1/4 (14-oz.) can Chinese pickled green
  vegetables, finely sliced
3 green onions, finely chopped
3 gingerroot slices
3-1/4 cups water
1-1/2 teaspoons rice wine or dry sherry
1 tablespoon light soy sauce
2 tofu cakes, finely sliced (8 ounces)
1 tablespoon Cornstarch Mixture, page 10
1 teaspoon sesame oil

Drain mushrooms, discard stalks, squeeze
out all the liquid, then slice very finely.

In a medium saucepan, bring all the ingredients except Cornstarch Mixture and
sesame oil to a boil; cook 3 minutes. Stir
in Cornstarch Mixture, simmer, still stirring, until thickened, then add sesame oil.

Makes 4 servings.

— ASPARAGUS & BEEF SOUP —

4 cups Chinese Chicken Stock, page 29
2 tablespoons rice wine or dry sherry
1-1/2 teaspoons sea salt
2 tablespoons Cornstarch Mixture, page 10
4 ounces beef tenderloin, very thinly sliced
White pepper
1/2 cup chopped asparagus tips
2 egg whites, lightly beaten

In a large saucepan, bring chicken stock, 1 tablespoon rice wine or dry sherry and 1/2 teaspoon salt to a boil. Reduce heat so the liquid barely simmers and stir in Cornstarch Mixture. Bring to a boil, stirring and boil until thickened. Reduce heat so liquid simmers.

Season steak with 1 teaspoon salt, 1 tablespoon rice wine or dry sherry and pepper. Add asparagus and steak to the stock and cook 10 minutes. Return to a boil and stir in egg whites in a thin stream.

Makes 4 servings.

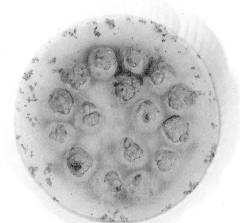

MEATBALL SOUP

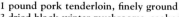

1 pound pork tenderloin, finely ground
3 dried black winter mushrooms, soaked in hot
    water 25 minutes, drained and finely chopped
2 green onions, very finely chopped
2 tablespoons light soy sauce
Sea salt
2/3 cup cornstarch for coating
3 tablespoons peanut oil
7 cups Chinese Chinese Chicken Stock, page 29,
    plus 1 cup water
1/2 teaspoon ground black pepper
Chopped parsley, to garnish

In a bowl, mix together pork, mushrooms, green onions, soy sauce and 1 teaspoon salt. Pass through the finest blade of a grinder. Roll mixture into 1-inch balls. Roll balls in cornstarch to lightly coat.

In a wok, heat oil and fry meatballs about 4 minutes until lightly and evenly browned. Drain on paper towels. In a saucepan, heat chicken stock and water to a boil. Reduce heat so stock simmers, then add meatballs. Season with salt and pepper. Garnish with chopped parsley.

Makes 4 servings.

CRISPY SEAWEED

1-3/4 cups tender collard greens or spinach
2-1/2 cups vegetable oil
1 tablespoon brown sugar
1/2 teaspoon sea salt
1/2 teaspoon ground cinnamon
3/4 cup sliced almonds, to garnish,
   if desired

Remove the thick ribs from the leaves and discard.

Wash greens, drain and dry thoroughly with paper towels. Using a very sharp knife or Chinese cleaver cut the leaves into very fine shreds. In a wok heat oil until smoking, then remove from heat and add greens. Return to medium heat and stir 2 to 3 minutes, or until the shreds begin to float.

Using a slotted spoon remove shreds from the oil and drain on paper towels. In a small bowl, mix together sugar, salt and cinnamon. Place 'seaweed' on a dish and sprinkle with the sugar mixture. Serve cold garnished with sliced almonds, if desired.

Makes 4 servings.

SHRIMP TOASTS

2 tablespoons finely ground pork fat
6 ounces peeled uncooked shrimp, finely ground
1/4 teaspoon sea salt
1 tablespoon cornstarch
1 egg white, lightly beaten
White pepper
3 thin white bread slices, crusts removed
2/3 cup sesame seeds
2-1/2 cups vegetable oil

In a bowl, mix together fat, shrimp, salt, cornstarch and egg white. Season with white pepper.

Spread on one side of each bread slice. Coat with a thick layer of sesame seeds, and press well into the spread. Cut each slice into 4 triangles.

In a wok, heat oil until smoking, reduce heat slightly, then carefully add the fingers, coated-side down. Deep-fry 2 to 3 minutes until golden brown. Drain on paper towels. Serve hot.

Makes 4 servings.

CHICKEN LIVERS WITH SHRIMP SAUCE

8 ounces chicken livers, washed
8 ounces uncooked shrimp in shells
1/4 cup Chinese rose wine or sweet sherry
2 tablespoons vegetable oil
1 fresh hot green chile, seeded if desired, finely
    sliced
1-inch piece gingerroot, peeled and grated
1 teaspoon yellow bean paste
1 tablespoon Cornstarch Mixture, page 10

Bring a small saucepan of water to a boil, add livers and cook 2 minutes. Drain, cool and slice. Shell and devein shrimp (page 19). Place shells in a saucepan with 1 cup water and simmer 30 minutes. Stir in wine or sweet sherry, strain and reserve liquid.

In a wok, heat oil, add chile and gingerroot and fry 30 seconds. Add livers and stir-fry 3 to 4 minutes. Using a slotted spoon, remove liver mixture from wok and drain on paper towels. Add shrimp to wok and stir-fry 2 minutes, then return livers, chile and gingerroot to wok and cook 2 minutes. Stir in reserved shrimp liquid and bean paste and simmer 5 minutes. Stir in Cornstarch Mixture and bring to a boil, stirring. Stir until bubbly.

Makes 4 servings.

—— SWEET & SOUR TOFU ——

12 ounces tofu, drained
2 egg whites
2 green onions, finely chopped
1 teaspoon sesame oil
Sea salt and white pepper
1/2 teaspoon brown sugar
1 (8-oz.) can water chestnuts, chopped
4 dried black winter mushrooms, soaked in hot
    water 25 minutes, drained and finely chopped
1 teaspoon finely chopped carrot, if desired
1 cup cornstarch, plus 2 tablespoons cornstarch
    for coating
2-1/2 cups peanut oil
2 green onions, chopped, to serve

Sauce:
1 tablespoon tomato paste
2 tablespoons rice vinegar
2 tablespoons fresh orange juice
2 teaspoons light soy sauce
5 teaspoons brown sugar

In a food processor or blender, process
tofu, then work in 1 egg white, the green
onions, sesame oil, salt, pepper and sugar.
Add water chestnuts, mushrooms, carrot,
if desired, remaining egg white and the 1
cup of cornstarch and mix well.

Transfer to a greased 6-inch cake pan,
leveling surface roughly. Place in a steaming basket, cover basket, place over a wok
or saucepan of boiling water and steam 10
minutes until firm. Cool.

Cut into bite-size pieces, toss in cornstarch to coat evenly and lightly.

In a wok, heat oil, add tofu pieces and deep-fry 5 minutes until golden. Drain on paper towels, place on a warmed serving plate and keep warm.

Pour oil from wok, leaving just 1 tablespoon. Stir in sauce ingredients and bring to a boil. Pour over tofu and sprinkle with chopped green onions.

Makes 4 servings.

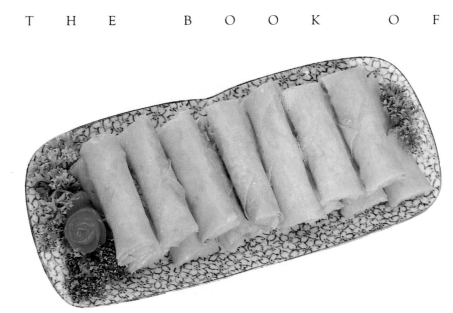

SPRING ROLLS

20 Spring Roll Skins, page 22
4 cups vegetable oil

Filling:
3 tablespoons peanut oil
50 mung bean sprouts
6 green onions, thinly shredded
1 cup julienned carrots
2 cups thinly sliced button mushrooms
1 garlic clove, very finely chopped
1 tofu cake, finely chopped
1/4 teaspoon Chinese five-spice powder
1 tablespoon light soy sauce
1 teaspoon sea salt

To make the filling, in a wok heat peanut oil and stir-fry vegetables, garlic and tofu about 1 minute. Add five-spice powder, soy sauce and salt and continue stir-frying 2 minutes. Cool.

Make the rolls, page 22.

In a wok or fryer, heat vegetable oil until smoking. Reduce heat slightly, add 4 spring rolls and fry 4 minutes, until crisp and golden. Drain on paper towels. Keep warm. Reheat oil, and cook 4 more spring rolls. Repeat with remaining rolls.

Variation: Substitute 1 cup chopped, prepared shrimp, page 19, in place of the tofu.

Makes 4 servings.

— PEKING CHICKEN WINGS —

12 chicken wings
2 cups peanut oil
1/2 cup Chinese Chicken Stock, page 29
2 green onions, finely chopped
1 tablespoon oyster sauce
1 tablespoon Cornstarch Mixture, page 10

Marinade:
1 tablespoon dark soy sauce
1 tablespoon peanut oil
1 tablespoon Chinese rose wine or sweet sherry
1/2-inch piece gingerroot, peeled and grated
2 garlic cloves, peeled and crushed

Place the wings in a saucepan, cover with water, bring to a simmer and cook 20 minutes. Drain and place in a dish. In a small bowl, mix together marinade ingredients. Pour over chicken wings. Let stand 1 hour, then drain thoroughly; reserve the marinade.

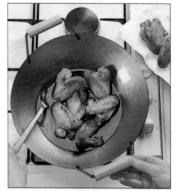

In a wok, heat oil, add wings and deep-fry 10 minutes until golden brown. Using a slotted spoon, remove wings from oil and drain on paper towels.

Pour oil from wok, then add chicken wings, stock, green onions, reserved marinade and oyster sauce. Gently cook 5 minutes. Stir in Cornstarch Mixture, bring to a boil, stirring, and simmer until thickened.

Makes 4 servings.

CLAMS WITH SOY & SESAME DIP

2 pounds clams in shells, scrubbed and rinsed
1 teaspoon sea salt
4 green onions, finely chopped
1-1/2-inch piece gingerroot, peeled and finely
    chopped
4 tablespoons dark soy sauce
1 teaspoon medium-dry sherry
2 tablespoons sesame oil

Bring a large saucepan of salted water to a rapid boil, add clams and boil 10 minutes until clams have opened. Discard any clams that do not open. Drain, remove and discard the top shells. Sprinkle each clam with green onions and gingerroot.

In a bowl mix together the soy, sherry and sesame oil. Spoon a little over each clam.

Makes 4 servings.

— DEEP-FRIED CRAB CLAWS —

4 large crab claws
10 ounces peeled uncooked shrimp, page 19,
  ground
1/2 teaspoon sea salt
Pinch of white pepper
1 teaspoon cornstarch
1 egg white
1 cup dried white bread crumbs to coat
2-1/2 cups peanut oil

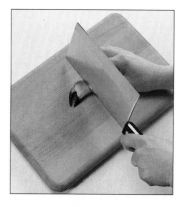

Crack and remove the main shell from each claw, leaving the pincer part intact. Bring a large saucepan of salted water to a boil. Add crab claws, return to a boil and boil 1 minute. Drain and refresh under cold running water.

In a bowl, mash to an even paste the shrimp, salt, pepper, cornstarch and egg white. Divide into 4 portions and press a portion around each claw, leaving pincer showing.

Place bread crumbs on a plate, roll claws in bread crumbs to evenly coat. In a wok, heat oil, add claws and fry 10 minutes until golden brown. Drain on paper towels.

Makes 4 servings.

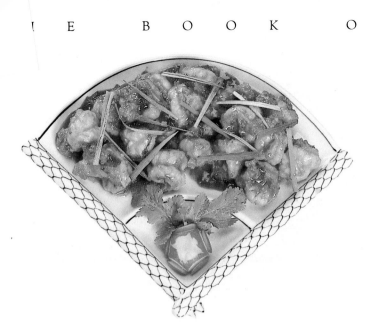

KUNG PO SHRIMP

1 pound prepared raw shrimp, page 19
5 or 6 tablespoons water
4 tablespoons cornstarch
2-1/2 cups peanut oil
2 green onions, finely chopped
1/2-inch piece gingerroot, peeled and finely
    chopped
1 tablespoon rice wine or dry sherry
1 tablespoon light soy sauce
1 teaspoon brown sugar
2 teaspoons sherry vinegar
Sea salt and black pepper

In a bowl, stir water into cornstarch to
make a light batter. Dip shrimp in batter
to coat evenly; allow excess batter to drain
off.

In a wok, heat oil until smoking, add
shrimp and deep-fry about 3 minutes
until golden brown. Using a slotted
spoon, remove and then drain on paper
towels. Pour oil from wok, leaving just 2
tablespoonsful. Add green onions and
ginger and stir-fry 1 minute. Stir in
remaining ingredients and bring to a boil.
Add shrimp to sauce and heat gently until
sauce has thickened.

Makes 4 servings.

PHOENIX SHRIMP

8 large uncooked shrimp, peeled, page 19
1-inch piece gingerroot, peeled and grated
3 green onions, chopped
2 tablespoons rice wine or dry sherry
1 teaspoon sesame oil
1 tablespoon light soy sauce
1/2 teaspoon sea salt
About 3/4 cup dry bread crumbs for coating
2-1/2 cups vegetable oil

Batter:
4 egg whites
2 tablespoons cornstarch
2 tablespoons all-purpose flour

Using a cleaver or large knife slightly flatten shrimp along their length; place in a dish. In a bowl, mix together gingerroot, green onions, rice wine or dry sherry, sesame oil, soy sauce and salt. Pour over shrimp and let stand 30 minutes. Make batter in a bowl by beating together the egg whites until stiff, then beat in the cornstarch and flour.

Dip shrimp in batter to coat thickly and evenly, then coat well with dry bread crumbs.

In a wok heat vegetable oil until very hot, add shrimp and deep-fry 5 minutes until golden. Drain on paper towels.

Makes 4 servings.

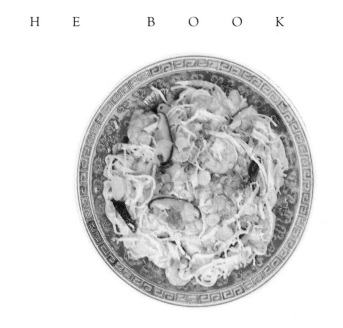

SHRIMP CHOW MEIN

8 ounces dried egg noodles
2 eggs, beaten
2 tablespoons vegetable oil
1 medium onion, sliced
10 canned water chestnuts, sliced
6 dried black winter mushrooms, soaked in hot
    water 20 minutes, drained and squeezed
1/2 cup Chinese Vegetable Stock, page 30
1-1/3 cups Chinese cabbage
1 pound shelled cooked shrimp
1 to 2 tablespoons Cornstarch Mixture, page 10

Boil egg noodles in salted water according to package instructions, drain and keep warm. Meanwhile, use the eggs to make 2 thin Chinese Omelets, page 24.

In a wok heat oil, add onion, water chestnuts and mushrooms, and stir-fry 3 minutes. Stir in stock and cabbage and cook 3 minutes. Add shrimp. Stir in Cornstarch Mixture, bring to a boil, stirring, and simmer until thickened. Place noodles in a warmed bowl, top with shrimp and vegetables. Thinly slice omelets and scatter over shrimp and vegetables.

Makes 4 servings.

SZECHUAN SHRIMP

1 pound shelled uncooked shrimp, page 19
2 tablespoons vegetable oil
1 garlic clove, finely chopped
1 small fresh red chile, seeded if desired, finely
   chopped
1-1/2 teaspoons chili sauce
1/4 teaspoon cornstarch
2 tablespoons Chinese Chicken Stock, page 29
1/4 teaspoon brown sugar
1/4 teaspoon sea salt

Bring a large saucepan of salted water to a boil, add shrimp, boil 1 minute then drain. In a wok, heat oil, garlic and chile and stir-fry 30 seconds. Add chili sauce and stir 3 minutes.

In a small bowl mix together cornstarch, stock, sugar and salt until smooth, then stir into the wok. Bring to a boil, stirring, then simmer until sauce is thick. Add shrimp and gently heat through about 2 minutes.

Makes 4 servings.

MUSSELS WITH BEANS & CHILE

8 pounds mussels, scrubbed and rinsed
1/2 cup vegetable oil
4 garlic cloves, finely chopped
2 hot red chiles, seeded if desired, finely
    chopped
1/2 green bell pepper, chopped
3 green onions, sliced
1 tablespoon Cornstarch Mixture, page 10
4 tablespoons rice wine or dry sherry
3 tablespoons black bean paste
2 teaspoons ground ginger
1 tablespoon brown sugar
2 tablespoons hot chile paste
3 tablespoons oyster sauce
3 cups Chinese Chicken Stock, page 29

Place mussels in a large saucepan, add 2 cups water, cover and place over a high heat about 5 minutes, shaking pan occasionally, or until the mussels have opened. This may have to be done in batches. Remove from heat, drain and discard any mussels which have not opened.

In a wok, heat oil, add garlic, chiles, green pepper and green onions and stir-fry 1 minute. In a bowl stir together remaining ingredients, stir into wok and bring to a boil, stirring. Simmer until lightly thickened.

Add mussels to wok and heat through 5 minutes, occasionally shaking wok.

Makes 4 to 6 servings.

SCALLOPS WITH BLACK BEANS

12 scallops on their half-shells
2 tablespoons peanut oil
2 garlic cloves, finely chopped
3 green onions, finely chopped
1 fresh hot green chile, seeded and chopped
3 tablespoons fermented salted black beans,
    soaked 20 minutes, drained
2 tablespoons dark soy sauce
2 teaspoons brown sugar
3 tablespoons Chinese Chicken Stock, page 29
2 teaspoons cornstarch

Place the scallops on their shells in a
steaming basket, place over a wok or
saucepan of boiling water. Cover and
cook 6 minutes.

Meanwhile, in a wok, heat oil, add garlic,
green onions, chile and black beans and
stir-fry 2 minutes, mashing the beans. Stir
in soy sauce and sugar 1 to 2 minutes.

Blend the stock with the cornstarch until smooth. Stir into wok, bring to a
boil, stirring, and simmer until thickened.
Keep warm.

Transfer scallops to a warmed serving
plate and spoon a little sauce over each.

Makes 4 servings.

— SEA TREASURES STIR-FRY —

2 tablespoons cornstarch
1 egg white
6 ounces peeled uncooked shrimp, page 19
6 ounces cleaned squid, page 20
6 ounces scallops, sliced
2 tablespoons peanut oil
2 celery stalks, chopped
1 medium carrot, thinly sliced
1-inch piece gingerroot, peeled and finely
    chopped
3 garlic cloves, finely chopped
4 green onions, finely chopped
1/2 cup Chinese Chicken Stock, page 29
1 teaspoon sea salt
1 tablespoon rice wine or dry sherry
1 teaspoon rice vinegar

In a bowl mix together cornstarch and egg white to make a light batter. Separately, dip shrimp, squid and scallops into batter to coat evenly; allow excess batter to drain off. Reserve any remaining batter.

In a wok, heat oil, add shrimp, scallops, squid, celery and carrot, fry about 3 minutes, then drain on paper towels. Pour oil from wok, leaving just 1 tablespoon. Stir in remaining ingredients and bring to a boil. Reduce heat so sauce simmers, add seafood and vegetables and stir gently 2 minutes. If sauce is thin, stir in 1 teaspoon reserved batter to thicken.

Makes 4 servings.

1 (3-lb.) lobster
2 tablespoons peanut oil
1/2 inch piece gingerroot, peeled and grated
4 green onions, coarsely chopped
1 teaspoon sea salt
3/4 cup Chinese Chicken Stock, page 29
2 tablespoons dark soy sauce
2 tablespoons rice wine or dry sherry

Insert the point of a large, heavy knife in the back of the head of the lobster, then move the knife towards the tail in a series of cutting movements, to split the lobster in half. Carefully remove head and black intestinal thread; discard. Crack the claws.

In a wok, over a medium heat, heat oil, add lobster pieces, cover and cook 4 minutes. Remove and drain on paper towels. Pour oil from wok leaving just 1 tablespoon. Stir remaining ingredients into the wok and bring to a boil. Return lobster pieces to wok, cover and simmer 5 minutes. Transfer lobster to a warmed serving plate and pour sauce over lobster.

Makes 4 servings.

SQUID STIR-FRY

1-1/2 pounds cleaned squid, page 20
3 tablespoons vegetable oil
4 green onions, chopped
1 garlic clove, finely chopped
1/2-inch piece gingerroot, peeled and finely
**   chopped**
1 carrot, cut into thin strips
5 tablespoons rice wine or dry sherry
3/4 cup Chinese Chicken Stock, page 29

Bring a large saucepan of lightly salted water to a rapid boil, add squid and boil 3 minutes. Drain well.

In a wok, heat oil, add green onions, garlic, gingerroot and carrot and stir-fry 2 minutes. Stir in rice wine or dry sherry and cook 1 minute. Pour in the stock, bring to a boil, and boil until reduced. Reduce heat, add squid and gently heat through.

Makes 4 servings.

SQUID FLOWERS WITH PEPPERS

2-1/2 cups peanut oil
1 pound cleaned squid, page 20
2 slices gingerroot, peeled and finely chopped
1 large green bell pepper, cut into squares
1 teaspoon sea salt
1 tablespoon dark soy sauce
1 teaspoon rice vinegar
1/2 teaspoon brown sugar
Black pepper
1 teaspoon sesame oil

In a wok, heat oil until smoking, add squid and fry 1 minute. Remove and drain on paper towels. Pour oil from wok, leaving just 1 tablespoon. Add gingerroot and green bell pepper and stir-fry 5 minutes until the bell pepper begins to soften.

Stir in remaining ingredients except sesame oil, bring to a boil, stirring, reduce heat so sauce is simmering, then add squid and gently heat through. Transfer to a warmed serving plate and sprinkle with sesame oil.

Makes 4 servings.

— YELLOW RIVER CARP —

1 (2-lb.) carp, ready to cook
2 teaspoons sea salt
2 tablespoons all-purpose flour
2 tablespoons cornstarch
5 or 6 tablespoons cold water
2-1/2 cups peanut oil

Sauce:
1 tablespoon cornstarch
2 tablespoons brown sugar
4 tablespoons rice vinegar
1 tablespoon dark soy sauce
2 tablespoons rice wine or dry sherry
6 tablespoons water

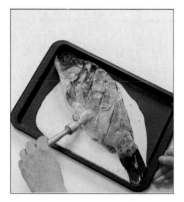

Make 3 diagonal cuts in one direction, on
each side of fish. Make 3 more cuts on
each side, in the opposite direction, to
make a diamond pattern. Sprinkle inside
and out with salt. Mix together flour and
cornstarch, then gradually stir in enough
water to make a light batter. Pour and
brush over fish until evenly coated; allow excess to drain off. In a wok, heat
oil, carefully add fish and fry about 10
minutes until an even light golden-brown.
Remove fish, drain on paper towels, then
place on a warmed serving plate, keep
warm. Reserve oil.

To make the sauce, in a small saucepan,
heat 2 tablespoons of the reserved oil. In
a small bowl, mix together all ingredients.
Pour into the saucepan and cook over
medium heat, stirring, until thickened.
Pour over fish.

Makes 4 servings.

——— DRUNKEN FISH ———

2 tablespoons cornstarch
1 teaspoon sea salt
1 pound haddock or other firm white fish fillets,
    thinly sliced
1 egg white, lightly beaten
2-1/2 cups vegetable oil
2 tablespoons peanut oil
12 dried black winter mushrooms soaked in hot
    water 25 minutes, drained

Sauce:
1 tablespoon Cornstarch Mixture, page 10
1/4 cup Chinese Chicken Stock, page 29
5 tablespoons rice wine or dry sherry
1-1/2 teaspoons brown sugar

On a plate, mix together cornstarch and salt, coat fish slices evenly, shaking off any excess, then dip fish slices separately into the egg white to coat; allow excess to drain off. In a wok, over medium heat, heat vegetable oil, add fish and cook 2 minutes on each side; the fish should remain white. Remove, drain on paper towels and keep warm. Pour oil from wok. In a medium saucepan, heat peanut oil, add mushrooms and stir-fry 1 minute. Drain on paper towels.

For the sauce, in a bowl, mix together ingredients, stir into wok, bring to a boil, then simmer until sauce thickens. Gently stir in fish to coat. To serve, place mushrooms on a serving dish, top with the fish slices and sauce.

Makes 4 servings.

— BAKED RED SNAPPER —

1 (2-lb.) whole red snapper, ready to cook
1 teaspoon ground ginger
1 teaspoon sea salt
1 teaspoon black pepper
1 onion, sliced into rings
1-inch piece gingerroot, peeled and finely
    chopped
1-1/2 teaspoons salted (fermented) black beans,
    soaked 20 minutes, drained
1 tablespoon rice wine or dry sherry
1 tablespoon soy sauce
1 teaspoon brown sugar
2 tablespoons peanut oil

Preheat oven to 350F (175C).

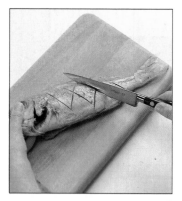

Using a sharp knife, cut both sides diagonally in one direction, then in the opposite direction to give a diamond pattern. In a small bowl, mix together ground ginger, salt and pepper. Rub into both sides of fish and sprinkle some inside. Cut a piece of cooking foil large enough to enclose fish completely; lay on a baking sheet.   Arrange onion and gingerroot on one half of foil. Top with fish.

Mash black beans, rice wine or dry sherry, soy sauce and sugar together, then spread over fish. Heat oil until smoking and pour over the fish. Fold foil over fish and seal seams tightly. Bake 20 minutes until the fish turns from translucent to opaque. Serve topped with the cooking juices.

Makes 4 servings.

— FISH WITH GREEN ONIONS —

1 (2-lb.) whole red snapper, sea bass or trout,
  ready to cook
1-1/2 teaspoons sea salt
2 teaspoons sesame oil
1/2-inch piece gingerroot, peeled and finely
  chopped
10 green onions, coarsely chopped
2 garlic cloves, finely chopped
1/2 teaspoon ground white pepper
5 teaspoons rice vinegar
1 tablespoon brown sugar
2 tablespoons dark soy sauce
1 cup water

Sprinkle fish inside and out with salt. Let
stand 15 minutes, then rinse and pat dry
with paper towels. In a wok, heat sesame
oil, add gingerroot and stir 30 seconds.
Add fish and fry gently 2 minutes on each
side, then remove and drain on paper
towels and keep warm.

Add half the green onions to the wok,
place fish on top, then cover with
remaining green onions. In a bowl mix
together remaining ingredients, pour over
fish and bring to a boil. Reduce heat so
liquid barely simmers, cover and cook 45
minutes until the fish turns from translucent to opaque.

Makes 4 servings.

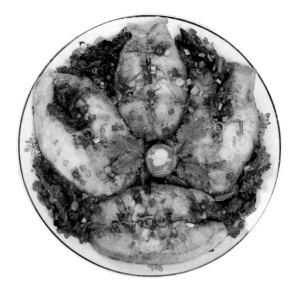

— HUNAN FISH STEAKS —

2-1/2 cups vegetable oil
4 cod steaks, 6 ounces each
4 green onions, chopped, to serve
2 teaspoons sesame oil, to serve

Sauce:
4 dried black winter mushrooms, soaked in hot
    water 25 minutes, drained
2 medium onions, finely chopped
3 gingerroot slices, peeled and finely chopped
2 garlic cloves, finely chopped
2 tablespoons Chinese radish pickle, chopped
3 dried red chiles
3/4 cup Chinese Chicken Stock, page 29
3 tablespoons dark soy sauce
2 tablespoons brown sugar
2 teaspoons sea salt
4 tablespoons rice wine or dry sherry

In a wok, heat oil until just smoking. Add
fish steaks 2 at a time and deep fry 1-1/2
minutes each side; remove, drain on paper
towels and keep warm. Reheat oil before
adding the other steaks. Pour oil from
wok, leaving just 3 tablespoons. Stir in
sauce ingredients and boil, stirring until
reduced by half.

Reduce heat so sauce is just simmering,
add fish steaks and heat through gently,
turning occasionally, 5 minutes. Transfer
fish to a warmed serving plate, pour over
sauce, sprinkle with finely chopped green
onions and sesame oil.

Makes 4 servings.

—— STEAMED SEA BASS ——

1 (2-lb.) whole sea bass, snapper or trout, ready
    to cook
2 tablespoons lemon juice
6 green onions, shredded lengthways

Marinade:
1 tablespoon dark soy sauce
1 tablespoon cornstarch
1 tablespoon rice wine or dry sherry
1/2 teaspoon ground ginger
1/2 teaspoon black pepper

Sauce:
1 tablespoon Chinese Chicken Stock, page 29
2 tablespoons rice wine or dry sherry
1 teaspoon brown sugar
1/2 teaspoon sea salt
1/3 cup peanut oil
2 small leeks, white part only, very finely sliced
1/2-inch piece gingerroot, peeled and grated

With the point of a sharp knife, make 4
diagonal cuts on each side of fish.
Sprinkle inside and out with lemon juice.
Place in a dish that will fit inside a
steamer, curving the fish as necessary.   In
a small bowl, mix together marinade
ingredients. Pour over fish, turn to coat
with marinade; let stand 1 hour. Place the
dish in a steamer, cover, place over boiling
water and cook 20 minutes.

To make the sauce, in a saucepan, mix
together stock, rice wine, sugar and salt;
simmer 4 minutes. Remove from heat.
In a wok, heat oil, add leeks and
gingerroot and gently stir-fry 2 to 3
minutes.   Stir in contents of saucepan;
heat through. Transfer fish to a warmed
serving dish, pour over sauce and sprinkle
with shredded green onions.

Makes 4 servings.

– FISH STIR-FRY WITH GINGER –

1/2 cup cornstarch
1/2 teaspoon ground ginger
1 teaspoon sea salt
1-1/2 pounds haddock or other firm white fish
  fillets, skinned and cubed
3 tablespoons peanut oil
1-inch piece gingerroot, peeled and finely
  chopped
4 green onions, thinly sliced
1 tablespoon ChingKiang vinegar or red wine
  vinegar
2 tablespoons rice wine or dry sherry
3 tablespoons dark soy sauce
1 teaspoon sugar
3 tablespoons fresh orange juice

In a bowl, mix together cornstarch, ground ginger and salt, add fish in batches to coat evenly.

In a wok, heat oil. Add fish and fry 4 minutes, occasionally turning gently, until evenly browned. In a bowl, mix together remaining ingredients, stir into wok, reduce the heat so the liquid just simmers, cover and cook 4 minutes.

Makes 4 servings.

SNAPPER IN HOT BEAN SAUCE

1 cup peanut oil
1 (2-lb.) red snapper, porgy or trout, ready to cook
4 garlic cloves, finely chopped
2 tablespoons hot bean sauce
3/4 cup Chinese Chicken Stock, page 29
1 tablespoon red wine vinegar
1 tablespoon rice wine or dry sherry
3 slices gingerroot, peeled and finely chopped
1 tablespoon dark soy sauce
1/2 teaspoon sea salt
1-1/2 teaspoons cornstarch
3 green onions, finely chopped, to garnish

In a wok heat oil. Add fish and fry 4 minutes on each side until just beginning to brown. Remove, drain on paper towels and keep warm. Pour oil from wok, leaving just 2 tablespoons. Add garlic, stir-fry 30 seconds, then add hot bean sauce and stir a further 30 seconds.

Stir in remaining ingredients, except green onions, and bring to a boil, stirring. Reduce heat, add fish, bring to simmer, cover and cook 25 minutes. Check frequently to make sure sauce is not drying out; if necessary stir in a little water. Transfer fish to a warmed plate, top with sauce and garnish with finely chopped green onions.

Makes 4 servings.

SWEET & SOUR FISH

1/2 teaspoon sea salt
2 tablespoons cornstarch
4 haddock fillets, 6 ounces each
1 egg white, beaten
2-1/2 cups vegetable oil

Sauce:
1 tablespoon brown sugar
2 tablespoons rice vinegar
1 tablespoon Chinese Chicken Stock, page 29
1 tablespoon chili sauce
2 tablespoons fresh orange juice
1 tablespoon Cornstarch Mixture, page 10

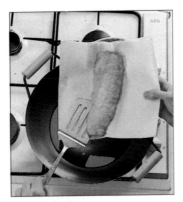

On a plate, mix together salt and cornstarch then coat fish evenly, shaking off any excess. Dip each fillet in egg white. In a wok, heat oil. Add fish and deep-fry 5 minutes until golden. Drain on paper towels and keep warm.

In a medium saucepan, mix together sauce ingredients, bring to a boil, stirring, then simmer 3 minutes. Transfer the fish to a warmed serving plate and pour sauce over fish.

Makes 4 servings.

CHICKEN IN BLACK BEAN SAUCE

1 cup peanut oil
1 pound boned chicken breasts, cubed
10 button mushrooms, halved
1/2 red bell pepper, diced
1/2 green bell pepper, diced
4 green onions, finely chopped
2 carrots, thinly sliced
2 tablespoons salted fermented black beans,
    rinsed
1/2-inch piece gingerroot, peeled and grated
1 garlic clove, finely chopped
2 tablespoons rice wine or dry sherry
1 cup Chinese Vegetable Stock, page 30
1 tablespoon light soy sauce
2 tablespoons Cornstarch Mixture, page 10

In a wok, heat oil until smoking, add chicken cubes and deep-fry 2 minutes. Using a slotted spoon, lift chicken from oil and drain on paper towels. Pour oil from wok, leaving just 2 tablespoons.

Add mushrooms to wok and stir-fry 1 minute. Add bell peppers, green onions and carrots, stir-fry 3 minutes. In a bowl, mash black beans with gingerroot, garlic and rice wine or dry sherry, stir into wok then stir in stock and soy sauce. Cook another 2 minutes. Stir in Cornstarch Mixture and bring to a boil, stirring. Stir in chicken and heat through gently.

Makes 4 servings.

——— MANDARIN CHICKEN ———

1 pound boned chicken breasts, diced
2 cups peanut oil
2 dried red chiles, chopped
1 teaspoon Szechuan peppercorns
1/2 cup unsalted peanuts, skinned
4 slices gingerroot, peeled and finely chopped
2 garlic cloves, thinly sliced
3 green onions, finely chopped
2/3 cup Chinese Chicken Stock, page 29
1 tablespoon light soy sauce
1 teaspoon brown sugar
1 teaspoon rice vinegar
1-1/2 teaspoons cornstarch

Marinade:
1/2 teaspoon sea salt
1 tablespoon light soy sauce
1 tablespoon rice wine or dry sherry
1-1/2 teaspoons cornstarch

In a bowl, mix together marinade ingredients. Stir in chicken to coat evenly,
then let stand 1 hour.

In a wok, heat oil until smoking, add
chiles and peppercorns in a wire strainer
and deep-fry 1 minute. Drain on paper
towels and reserve. Reheat oil and deep-
fry chicken 5 minutes until firm, white
and cooked through. At last moment, add
peanuts in a small metal basket and fry a
few seconds until brown; drain on paper
towels.

Using a slotted spoon, remove chicken from oil and drain on paper towels. Pour oil from wok, leaving just 3 tablespoons.

Add gingerroot, garlic and green onions to wok and stir-fry 30 seconds. Add chicken, chiles and peppercorns and stir-fry 3 minutes. In a bowl mix together stock, soy sauce, sugar, rice vinegar and cornstarch; stir into the wok with the peanuts. Bring to a boil, stirring, then reduce heat and cook 1 or 2 minutes.

Makes 4 servings.

—— CRISPY SKIN CHICKEN ——

1 (3-lb.) chicken
Salt
1 tablespoon light maple syrup
4 tablespoons plus 1 teaspoon sea salt
3-1/2 teaspoons Chinese five-spice powder
2 tablespoons rice vinegar
3-3/4 cups vegetable oil

Bring a large saucepan of salted water to a boil. Add chicken, return to a boil, then remove pan from heat, cover tightly and leave the chicken in the water 30 minutes.

Drain chicken, pat dry with paper towels and refrigerate 12 hours. In a small bowl, mix together maple syrup, 1 teaspoon salt, 1/2 teaspoon five-spice powder and the rice vinegar. Brush over chicken and refrigerate 20 minutes. Repeat until all the coating is used. Refrigerate the chicken at least 4 hours to allow the coating to dry thoroughly on the skin.

Split chicken in half, through the breast. In a wok, heat oil, add chicken halves and deep-fry 5 minutes until golden brown. Lift chicken from oil and drain on paper towels. Cut into bite-sized pieces. In a small saucepan over a low heat, stir together remaining sea salt and remaining five-spice powder 2 minutes. Sprinkle over chicken.

Makes 4 servings.

FIVE-SPICE CHICKEN

2 cups peanut oil
1 tablespoon dark soy sauce
1 tablespoon brandy
1/2 teaspoon Chinese five-spice powder
1/2 teaspoon brown sugar
1/2-inch piece gingerroot, peeled and finely
    chopped
2 green onions, finely chopped
2 garlic cloves, finely chopped
1 pound boned chicken breasts, cubed
1 large egg, beaten
1/2 cup cornstarch

In a large bowl, mix together 2 tablespoons peanut oil, soy sauce, brandy, five-spice powder, sugar, gingerroot, onions and garlic. Stir in chicken cubes to coat evenly. Let stand 1 hour. Stir in beaten egg. Put cornstarch on a plate, roll each chicken cube in cornstarch until evenly coated.

In a wok, heat remaining oil over medium heat, add chicken and deep-fry 4 minutes. Increase heat and fry 2 minutes until golden and cooked through. Using a slotted spoon, lift chicken from oil and drain on paper towels.

Makes 4 servings.

STEAMED CHICKEN WITH MUSHROOMS

2 teaspoons rice wine or dry sherry
2 tablespoons light soy sauce
1/2 teaspoon sea salt
1 teaspoon sugar
2 tablespoons Chinese Chicken Stock, page 29
1 (14-oz) can straw mushrooms, drained, liquid
    reserved
1 pound boned chicken breasts, cubed
2 gingerroot slices, peeled and chopped
3 green onions, coarsely chopped

In a bowl, mix together rice wine or dry sherry, soy sauce, salt, sugar, stock and reserved mushroom liquid.

Place chicken in a heatproof baking dish with mushrooms. Add contents of bowl, then sprinkle with gingerroot and green onions; cover dish. Place in a steamer, cover and cook 10 minutes until chicken is firm and tender. Remove dish from steamer and pour off cooking liquid into a wok. Bring to the boil, simmer 2 to 3 minutes, then pour over the chicken.

Makes 6 servings.

—— DUCK IN LEMON JUICE ——

2 tablespoons water
1 tablespoon rice wine or dry sherry
1-inch piece gingerroot, peeled and grated
3 green onions, finely chopped
1 teaspoon sea salt
1 pound boned duck breasts, cut into finger-size
    pieces
2 eggs, well beaten
1 cup cornstarch
3 cups peanut oil
1 teaspoon sesame oil

Sauce:
1-1/2 cups Chinese Chicken Stock, page 29
3 tablespoons rice wine or dry sherry
4 tablespoons lemon juice
1 teaspoon brown sugar

In a bowl, mix together water, rice wine or dry sherry, gingerroot, green onions and salt. Stir in duck to coat evenly, then refrigerate 2 hours. Lift duck from bowl, then dip each piece in beaten egg, allowing excess to drain off. Roll duck pieces in cornstarch to coat lightly and evenly.

In a wok, heat peanut oil to smoking point, add duck and deep-fry 3 minutes until golden. Using a slotted spoon, remove duck from oil and drain on paper towels. Place duck in a saucepan. In a small bowl, mix together sauce ingredients; stir into duck. Bring to boil, stirring constantly, then simmer 10 to 15 minutes until duck is tender and sauce is very thick. Serve sprinkled with sesame oil.

Makes 4 servings.

PEKING DUCK

1 (4-lb.) oven-ready duck
1 tablespoon honey
3 tablespoons dark soy sauce
1 tablespoon sesame oil
Red food coloring, if desired
2 tablespoons water

Pancakes:
3-1/2 cups all-purpose flour
1 cup boiling water
1/3 cup cold water
1 teaspoon sesame oil

To serve:
Hoisin sauce
6 green onions, cut into long shreds
1/2 cucumber, cut into long shreds

Place the duck in a colander in the sink. Pour boiling water over; repeat twice. Hang duck overnight in a cold airy place, or place on a rack in the refrigerator. Next morning, in a small bowl, mix together honey, soy sauce, sesame oil and coloring, if used. Place duck on a rack in a roasting pan, making sure the neck opening is closed. Brush evenly with honey mixture and let stand 1 hour.

Preheat oven to 405F (205C).

Stir water into remaining honey mixture and pour through the vent, into the duck. With a meat skewer or wooden skewer, secure vent. Roast duck, 1-1/2 hours, until juices run clear. Remove duck from oven and leave in a warm place 10 minutes before carving.

Meanwhile, make the pancakes. Sift flour into a bowl and gradually stir in boiling water; mix well. Stir in cold water to form a ball. On a floured surface, knead until smooth. Return to bowl, cover with a damp cloth and let stand 15 minutes.

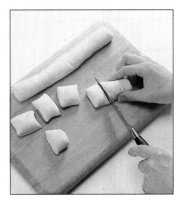

Divide dough in half; on a lightly floured surface, roll each half to a long roll 2 inches in diameter. Cut into 1-inch lengths. Flatten each piece with the palm of the hand. Lightly brush tops with sesame oil and place two pieces together, oiled-sides facing. Roll out each pair to 6-inch pancakes. Place a dry, non-stick skillet over medium heat and fry each pancake 20 to 30 seconds until beginning to bubble. Turn pancake over and cook a further 10 to 15 seconds until lightly browned.

Remove from skillet and carefully separate the top and bottom. Keep warm, interleaved with waxed paper.

Serve the carved duck on a warm plate with the stack of pancakes, and with hoisin sauce, green onions and cucumber in separate bowls.

Makes 4 servings.

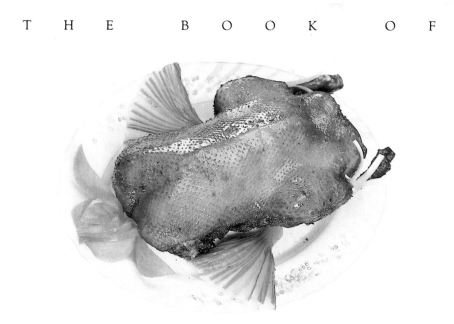

— SZECHUAN CRISPY DUCK —

5 cups Chinese Chicken Stock, page 29
1/2-inch piece gingerroot, peeled and sliced
3 tablespoons rice wine or dry sherry
1 tablespoon Szechuan peppercorns, lightly
    crushed
2 teaspoons sea salt
1/2 cup dark soy sauce
1/2 cup packed brown sugar
4 pieces star anise
1 (3-lb.) duck
3-3/4 cups peanut oil

In a large saucepan, mix together all ingredients except duck and oil and bring
to a boil. Add duck to liquid, return to
a boil, then reduce the heat so the liquid just simmers. Cook duck 2-1/2 to 3
hours. Drain duck; cool.

In a wok, heat oil until smoking, add duck
halves and deep-fry 5 minutes until crisp
and golden brown. Drain on paper towels
and serve as Peking Duck, page 72.

Makes 4 servings.

—— DUCK WITH LEEKS ——

4 tablespoons vegetable oil
2 leeks, thinly shredded
1 red bell pepper, sliced
1/2-inch piece gingerroot, peeled and thinly
    sliced
3 garlic cloves, finely chopped
2 tablespoons black bean paste
1 pound cooked boned duck, cut into strips
2-1/2 cups Chinese Stock, page 29
2 tablespoons light soy sauce
2 tablespoons rice vinegar
2 teaspoons brown sugar
2 teaspoons chili sauce

In a wok, heat oil until just smoking. Add
leeks, bell pepper, gingerroot and garlic.
Stir-fry briefly to coat with oil, then stir in
black bean paste and stir-fry 5 minutes until vegetables begin to soften.

Add duck and remaining ingredients and
stir-fry 2 to 3 minutes until duck is heated
through.

Makes 4 servings.

- DUCK WITH GREEN PEPPERS -

1 egg white
3 tablespoons cornstarch
Sea salt
1 pound boned duck breasts, cubed
2-1/2 cups peanut oil
2 green bell peppers, cut into 1-inch squares
2 tablespoons light soy sauce
3 teaspoons rice wine or dry sherry
1 teaspoon brown sugar
1/2 cup Chinese Chicken Stock, page 29
1 teaspoon sesame oil
White pepper

In a bowl, whisk together egg white, cornstarch and 1 teaspoon salt. Stir in duck cubes until coated. Let stand 20 minutes.

In a wok, heat peanut oil until very hot. Add duck and deep-fry 4 minutes, until crisp and golden. Remove duck and drain on paper towels. Add bell peppers to wok and deep-fry 2 minutes, then drain on paper towels. Pour oil from wok, leaving 2 tablespoons. Add soy sauce, rice wine or dry sherry, sugar, stock, sesame oil, salt and white pepper to taste. Bring to a boil, add cooked duck and bell peppers and gently heat through.

Makes 4 servings.

—— LAMB WITH CILANTRO ——

1 pound lean lamb, cut into thin strips
1 tablespoon cornstarch
1 teaspoon sugar
1 teaspoon sesame oil
2 tablespoons peanut oil
1-3/4 cups broccoli flowerets, sliced
3 dried black winter mushrooms, soaked in hot
    water 25 minutes, drained
2 green onions, chopped
1 garlic clove, finely chopped
2 teaspoons rice wine or dry sherry
1 tablespoon dark soy sauce
1 tablespoon finely chopped fresh cilantro

Place lamb in a dish. In a bowl, mix together cornstarch, sugar and sesame oil and stir into lamb until well coated. Let stand 30 minutes.

In a wok, heat peanut oil, add lamb and stir-fry 2 minutes. Remove lamb from wok and keep warm. Add broccoli, mushrooms, green onions and garlic and stir-fry about 5 minutes until broccoli is just tender. Stir in rice wine or dry sherry, soy sauce, lamb and cilantro. Stir over very high heat 1 minute.

Makes 4 servings.

LAMB CHOPS MONGOLIAN STYLE

1 tablespoon hoisin sauce
1 tablespoon dark soy sauce
2 garlic cloves, finely chopped
1 teaspoon sea salt
1/4 teaspoon white pepper
4 lamb chops, 6 to 8 ounces each
2 tablespoons peanut oil
2 medium onions, sliced
1/4 cup Chinese Vegetable Stock, page 30

Sauce:
1 fresh hot red chile, seeded and sliced
1 fresh hot green chile, seeded and sliced
1/2 teaspoon sea salt
1 tablespoon lemon juice
1 teaspoon brown sugar
2 tablespoons peanut oil

In a bowl, mix together hoisin sauce, soy sauce, garlic, salt and pepper. Coat chops with mixture and let stand 1 hour.

In a wok, heat oil until smoking, add onions and fry 2 minutes until transparent. Reduce heat, add chops and cook about 5 minutes each side. Add stock, cover and simmer 5 minutes. In a bowl, mix together all sauce ingredients, pour into a small saucepan and heat gently. Transfer chops to a warmed serving plate and top with sauce.

Makes 4 servings.

—— HUNAN LAMB STIR-FRY ——

1 egg white, lightly beaten
2 tablespoons cornstarch
Sea salt and white pepper to taste
1 pound lean lamb, thinly sliced
2-1/2 cups vegetable oil
3 slices gingerroot, peeled and finely chopped
1 (3-oz.) can sliced bamboo shoots or 1 (3-oz.)
    can bamboo shoots, drained and sliced if
    they come whole
1 small red bell pepper, cut into thin strips
3 green onions, finely chopped
1/4 cucumber, cut into strips
2 teaspoons rice wine or dry sherry

In a small bowl, mix together egg white, cornstarch, salt and pepper. Stir lamb slices in to mixture to evenly coat. Let stand 30 minutes.

In a wok, heat oil, add lamb in batches, keeping slices separate, and deep-fry lamb 2 minutes. Using a slotted spoon, remove lamb from oil and drain on paper towels. Pour oil from wok, leaving just 2 tablespoons. Add gingerroot, bamboo shoots, bell pepper, green onions and cucumber and stir-fry 4 minutes. Add lamb and toss over high heat 1 minute. Stir in rice wine or dry sherry.

Makes 4 servings.

— LAMB IN GARLIC SAUCE —

1 pound lean lamb, very thinly sliced
3 tablepoons dark soy sauce
5 tablespoons peanut oil
1 tablespoon rice wine or dry sherry
1/2 teaspoon sea salt
1/2 teaspoon ground Szechuan pepper
2 garlic cloves, chopped
8 green onions, chopped
1 tablespoon rice vinegar
2 tablespoons sesame oil

Lay lamb in a shallow dish. In a bowl, mix together 1 tablespoon soy sauce, 2 tablespoons peanut oil, the rice wine or dry sherry, salt and Szechuan pepper. Pour over lamb, turn to coat, then let stand 30 minutes.

In a wok, heat remaining peanut oil until smoking, add garlic and lamb. Stir-fry 2 minutes until lamb just changes color; remove from wok. Pour oil from wok, leaving just 1 tablespoon. Add green onions and stir-fry 2 minutes. Add remaining soy sauce and the vinegar. Continue stir-frying another minute, then add the lamb slices and sesame oil. Stir-fry 1 minute, making sure lamb and sauce are thoroughly mixed.

Makes 4 servings.

- LAMB WITH GREEN ONIONS -

1 egg white
1/2 cup cornstarch
1 teaspoon sea salt
1 tablespoon rice wine or dry sherry
1 pound lean lamb, cut into strips
1-1/4 cups vegetable oil
10 green onions, chopped
1/2-inch piece gingerroot, peeled and finely
   chopped
2 garlic cloves, finely chopped
1 teaspoon brown sugar
2 teaspoons dark soy sauce
1/4 teaspoon white pepper
1 teaspoon sesame oil, to serve

In a bowl, mix together egg white, cornstarch, 1/2 teaspoon salt, and rice wine or dry sherry. Stir in lamb strips to coat thoroughly.

In a wok, heat oil until smoking, add lamb in small batches, keeping strips separate and fry 2 minutes. Using a slotted spoon, remove lamb from wok, drain on paper towels and keep warm. Pour oil from wok, leaving just 1 tablespoon. Stir in green onions, gingerroot, garlic, remaining salt, sugar, soy sauce and pepper. Add lamb and heat through gently. Serve sprinkled with sesame oil.

Makes 4 servings.

– CHINESE BARBECUED LAMB –

2 small eggs, beaten
3/4 cup all-purpose flour
1 teaspoon sea salt
1/2 teaspoon black pepper
1 teaspoon ground Szechuan pepper
4 green onions, finely chopped
2 medium tomatoes, seeded and finely chopped
1 pound lean lamb, cut into cubes
4 teaspoons sesame seeds

In a bowl, mix together all ingredients, except lamb and sesame seeds. Stir in lamb to coat, cover and refrigerate 4 hours.

Preheat grill or barbecue. Spread sesame seeds on a plate. Roll lamb cubes in sesame seeds to coat evenly. Thread cubes on to skewers and sprinkle on any remaining sesame seeds. Broil or barbecue 4 or 5 minutes, turning frequently, until cooked.

Makes 4 servings.

— PORK WITH SNOW PEAS —

4 pork chops, 6 to 8 ounces each, boned and
   sliced thinly lengthwise.
1 teaspoon dark soy sauce
1 tablespoon yellow bean paste
2 tablespoons peanut oil
2 tablespoons Chinese rose wine or sweet sherry
2 carrots, sliced
8 ounces snow peas
2 garlic cloves, finely chopped
1-inch piece gingerroot, peeled and finely
   chopped

Place pork in a dish. In a small bowl,
mix together soy sauce, bean paste, 1
tablespoon peanut oil and rose wine or
sweet sherry, then pour over pork. Turn
slices to coat well and marinate 1 hour.
Drain and reserve marinade. Bring a
saucepan of water to a rapid boil, add
carrots and snow peas and boil 1 minute.
Drain and refresh under cold running
water.

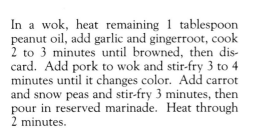

In a wok, heat remaining 1 tablespoon
peanut oil, add garlic and gingerroot, cook
2 to 3 minutes until browned, then discard. Add pork to wok and stir-fry 3 to 4
minutes until it changes color. Add carrot
and snow peas and stir-fry 3 minutes, then
pour in reserved marinade. Heat through
2 minutes.

Makes 4 servings.

—— CHAI SUI ROAST PORK ——

1 (1-lb.) pork tenderloin
2 tablespoons rice wine or dry sherry
3 tablespoons brown sugar
3 tablespoons peanut oil
1 tablespoon yellow bean paste
2 tablespoons dark soy sauce
2 tablespoons red fermented tofu

In a bowl, mix together all ingredients, except pork. Spoon over pork and leave at room temperature 1 hour.

Preheat oven to 400F (205C). Put tenderloin on a rack in a roasting pan and roast 15 to 20 minutes until juices run clear and outside is richly colored.

Makes 4 servings.

——— PORK WITH NOODLES ———

8 ounces dried egg noodles
3 tablespoons peanut oil
1 medium-size onion, finely chopped
2 garlic cloves, finely chopped
2 slices gingerroot, peeled and finely chopped
2 teaspoons yellow bean paste
1 tablespoon light soy sauce
1 pound ground lean pork
3 tablespoons Chinese Chicken Stock, page 29
1 tablespoon Cornstarch Mixture, page 10
1 small cucumber, cut into thin sticks, to garnish
3 green onions, finely chopped, to garnish

Cook noodles in boiling water until just tender, drain well.   Meanwhile, in a wok, heat oil, add onion, garlic and gingerroot and stir-fry 2 minutes.   Stir in bean paste and soy sauce; cook 1 minute.   Stir in pork, reduce heat and cook 10 minutes until lightly colored. Stir in stock and simmer 5 minutes.   Stir in Cornstarch Mixture and simmer until thickened.

To serve, place noodles on a warmed serving dish, pour over pork and garnish with cucumber and green onions.

Makes 4 servings.

— SWEET & SOUR PORK —

1/2 teaspoon sea salt
2 teaspoons rice wine or dry sherry
1 large egg, beaten
1 pound pork shoulder, cubed
1 cup cornstarch
2-1/2 cups peanut oil
3 green onions, thinly sliced
1 (14-oz) can bamboo shoots, drained and thinly
   sliced
1 green bell pepper, thinly sliced
2 garlic cloves, finely chopped
1 teaspoon sesame oil

Sauce:
2 tablespoons brown sugar
1 tablespoon vegetable oil
3 tablespoons malt vinegar
1 teaspoon cornstarch
Sea salt and white pepper

In a bowl, mix salt, rice wine or dry
sherry and egg. Stir in pork to evenly
coat. Remove pork and roll in cornstarch
to coat evenly. In a wok, heat peanut
oil until smoking and deep-fry pork 5
minutes until crisp. Using a slotted spoon,
remove pork from oil and drain on paper
towels. Pour oil from wok, leaving just 2
tablespoons.   Add vegetables and garlic
and stir-fry 3 minutes. Stir in pork and
mix thoroughly.

To make the sauce, in a saucepan, stir
together all ingredients and place over
medium heat 4 minutes, stirring constantly until hot and well blended. Pour
over pork and briefly heat together.
Sprinkle with sesame oil and serve.

Makes 4 servings.

SZECHUAN PORK

3 tablespoons vegetable oil
1/2 (14-oz) can Szechuan preserved cabbage,
    soaked 1 hour, drained and shredded
1 (1-lb.) pork tenderloin, very thinly sliced
3 green onions, finely chopped
3 slices gingerroot, peeled and finely chopped
1 fresh red chile, seeded and very finely sliced
1 red bell pepper, cut into strips
1 tablespoon light soy sauce
2 tablespoons rice wine or dry sherry
1/2 teaspoon brown sugar

In a wok, heat oil, add cabbage and pork and stir-fry 2 minutes until pork changes color. Stir in green onions, gingerroot, chile and bell pepper.

In a small bowl, mix together remaining ingredients. Stir into wok and cook 2 minutes.

Makes 4 servings.

BARBECUED PORK

1 (1-1/2-lb.) pork loin, cut into long strips
2/3 cup brown sugar
3 tablespoons boiling water
1 tablespoon dark soy sauce
1 tablespoon oyster sauce
2 tablespoons rice wine or dry sherry
1 teaspoon sesame oil
1/2 teaspoon sea salt
1/2 teaspoon red food coloring, if desired
Chinese shredded lettuce, to serve

Place pork in a medium bowl. In a small bowl, stir together sugar and boiling water until sugar dissolves, then stir in remaining ingredients except lettuce. Cool slightly, then pour over pork, turning pork several times to coat evenly. Refrigerate 8 hours, turning the pork several times. Lift pork from marinade, allowing excess to drain off; reserve.

Preheat grill or broiler. Thread meat on to meat skewers and barbecue or broil about 8 minutes until crisp and cooked, basting several times with reserved marinade.

To serve, remove the pork from the skewers, cut into bite-size pieces and serve on a bed of shredded Chinese lettuce.

Makes 4 to 6 servings.

—— PORK WITH CASHEWS ——

1 teaspoon rice wine or dry sherry
1/2 teaspoon sea salt
1 teaspoon sugar
2 teaspoons cornstarch
1 (1-lb.) pork tenderloin, cubed
2-1/2 cups peanut oil
3/4 cup cashews
3 garlic cloves, finely chopped
2 green onions, coarsely chopped
1/2 red bell pepper, seeded and diced
1/2 green pepper, seeded and diced
4 dried winter mushrooms, soaked in hot water
    25 minutes, drained

Sauce:
1 teaspoon light soy sauce
1/2 teaspoon sea salt
1/4 teaspoon white pepper
1 teaspoon cornstarch
1/3 cup Chinese Chicken Stock, page 29

In a bowl, mix together rice wine or dry sherry, salt, sugar and cornstarch. Stir in pork to coat evenly. Let stand 30 minutes. In a wok, heat oil until very hot, add pork and deep-fry 3 or 4 minutes until cooked through. Using a slotted spoon, remove pork and drain on paper towels.

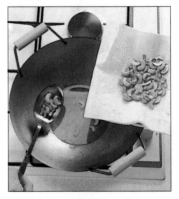

Add nuts to oil and deep-fry a few seconds until lightly colored. Remove with a slotted spoon. Drain on paper towels. Pour oil from wok, leaving just 1 tablespoon. Add garlic, fry briefly, then add all the vegetables. Continue cooking 3 to 4 minutes. In a bowl, mix together sauce ingredients, stir into wok and simmer until thickened. Stir in pork and heat through gently.

Makes 4 servings.

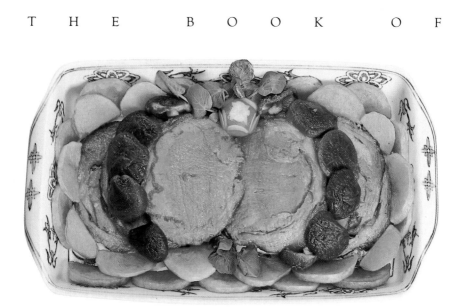

CHINESE ROAST BEEF

1 (3-lb.) sirloin roast beef
2 garlic cloves, thinly sliced
1/2 teaspoon Chinese five-spice powder
Sea salt
1/4 teaspoon black pepper
8 potatoes, quartered
12 dried black winter mushrooms, soaked in hot
    water 25 minutes, drained

Preheat oven to 400F (205C).

With the point of a sharp knife, cut small incisions in the beef and insert thin slices of garlic. In a bowl, mix together five-spice powder, 1 teaspoon salt and the pepper, then rub into beef. Place in a baking dish and roast 45 minutes, turning beef and basting at least once.

Boil potatoes in salted water 10 minutes. Drain well; when cool enough to handle, slice. Add to baking dish with mushrooms and cook 15 minutes.

Makes 8 servings.

— BOILED BEEF WITH CHILES —

1 (1-lb.) beef round steak, cut into paper thin
    slices
8 lettuce leaves, diced
1/2 teaspoon ground Szechuan pepper
1 garlic clove, finely chopped

Sauce:
2 tablespoons peanut oil
4 dried red chiles, crushed
1 teaspoon ground Szechuan pepper
1 tablespoon salted fermented black beans
4 green onions, coarsely chopped
2 garlic cloves, crushed
1/2-inch piece gingerroot, peeled and finely
    chopped
1 tablespoon hot bean paste
1/2-cup water

To make the sauce, in a wok, heat oil, add
chiles and pepper and fry 30 seconds, then
add black beans and cook 30 seconds.
Add green onions, garlic, gingerroot and
bean paste and fry 5 to 6 minutes. Stir in
water and bring to a boil, then remove
from the heat.

To prepare the beef, bring a large
saucepan of water to a rapid boil. Add
beef and boil 2 minutes until it just
changes color. Drain well. Reheat sauce
in the wok, add beef, stir 3 minutes, then
add the lettuce. Serve immediately
sprinkled with Szechuan pepper and finely
chopped garlic.

Makes 4 servings.

— BEEF WITH BELL PEPPERS —

4 tablespoons peanut oil
1-inch piece gingerroot, peeled and sliced thinly
1 (1-lb.) beef tenderloin, very thinly sliced
2 green bell peppers, seeded and cut into
    small squares

Sauce:
1/4 cup Chinese Vegetable Stock, page 30
1 tablespoon dark soy sauce
1 teaspoon sesame oil
1 fresh hot red chile, finely chopped
2 tablespoons Chinese rose wine
2 tablespoons Cornstarch Mixture, page 10

In a wok, heat oil, add gingerroot and fry
1 minute. Add beef and quickly stir-fry 2
minutes just until color changes. Stir in
bell peppers and stir-fry 5 minutes.

In a small bowl, mix together sauce ingredients. Stir into beef mixture; cook,
stirring until lightly thickened.

Makes 4 servings.

——— BEEF WITH CHOI SUM ———

1 (1-lb.) beef round steak, cut into thin strips
1/2 cup peanut oil
8 ounces choi sum or young spinach, washed
    and dried
Sea salt
1 teaspoon grated gingerroot
2 garlic cloves, finely chopped
4 green onions, coarsely chopped
2 teaspoons shrimp paste
1 teaspoon rice wine or dry sherry
1/2 teaspoon Cornstarch Mixture, page 10
1/4 cup Chinese Chicken Stock, page 29
1 teaspoon sesame oil

Marinade:
1 teaspoon dark soy sauce
1 teaspoon anchovy paste
1 tablespoon peanut oil
1 tablespoon cornstarch
1 teaspoon water

In a small bowl, mix together marinade
ingredients. Stir in steak to coat evenly.
Let stand 1 hour. In a wok, heat oil and
fry choi sum or spinach over high heat
2 minutes, sprinkle with salt and transfer
to a warmed serving plate. Keep warm.
Reheat wok and stir-fry beef 2 minutes
until it just changes color, then remove.
Add gingerroot, garlic and green onions
and stir-fry until tender, about 5 minutes.

In a small bowl, mix together shrimp
paste, rice wine or dry sherry, Cornstarch
Mixture and stock. Pour into wok and
bring to a boil, stirring. Stir in beef to
heat through.

Arrange beef and choi sum or spinach at-
tractively on the plate and sprinkle with
sesame oil.

Makes 4 servings.

— GREEN BEAN STIR-FRY —

4 teaspoons peanut oil
1 pound green beans, ends removed
1/2-inch piece gingerroot, peeled and grated
1/4 cup water
1 teaspoon brown sugar
1 teaspoon dark soy sauce
4 green onions, chopped

In a wok, heat 1 tablespoon oil, add beans and gingerroot and stir-fry 1 minute. Add water and sugar, reduce the heat and cook 5 to 6 minutes until beans are tender.

Stir in soy sauce then sprinkle with green onions and remaining oil.

Makes 4 servings.

— FAVA & BAMBOO SHOOTS —

8 ounces shelled fava beans
1 tablespoon vegetable oil
1 (8-oz.) can sliced bamboo shoots, drained
1 cup Chinese Chicken Stock, page 29
1 teaspoon sea salt
1 teaspoon Cornstarch Mixture, page 10
1 tablespoon sesame oil

Bring a saucepan of water to a boil, add fava beans and cook 8 minutes until their skins split. Drain and peel off skins.

In a wok, heat vegetable oil, add beans and bamboo shoots and stir-fry 2 minutes. Add stock and salt, cover and simmer 2 or 3 minutes. Stir in Cornstarch Mixture until thickened. Serve sprinkled with sesame oil.

Makes 4 servings.

CHOI SUM WITH FERMENTED TOFU

2 tablespoons vegetable oil
8 ounces Chinese flowering cabbage
1 (3-oz.) can fermented tofu
1 teaspoon toasted sesame seeds

In a wok, heat oil and fry cabbage 1 minute. Using a slotted spoon, remove from wok, drain on paper towels, then chop and arrange on a plate. Top with tofu and sprinkle with sesame seeds.

Makes 4 servings.

Note: Other Chinese cabbages could be substituted if the flowering variety is not available.

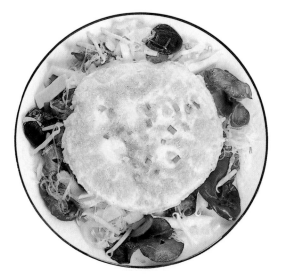

—— VEGETABLES IN A HAT ——

1/4 cup Chinese Chicken Stock, page 29
1 tablespoon rice wine or dry sherry
1/2 teaspoon sea salt
1/4 teaspoon sugar
2 ounces dried wood ear mushrooms, soaked in
    hot water 25 minutes, drained
4 dried black winter mushrooms, soaked in hot
    water 25 minutes, drained
4 ounces bean sprouts
1 (3-oz) can bamboo shoots, drained and finely
    chopped
1-1/4 cups shredded Chinese cabbage
4 ounces bean thread noodles, (see Note),
    soaked in hot water 25 minutes, drained
2 eggs, beaten

In a wok, bring chicken stock, rice wine
or dry sherry, salt and sugar to a boil.
Stir in mushrooms, bean sprouts, bamboo
shoots, cabbage and noodles, then simmer
8 minutes. Drain vegetables and noodles,
place in a warmed serving dish and keep
warm.

In a skillet, use the eggs to make Chinese
Omelet, page 24. Place the omelet on the
vegetables and serve immediately.

Makes 4 servings.

Note: Bean thread noodles are also
known as transparent noodles. Their
distinctive characteristic is that they do
not become mushy even after prolonged
cooking. Soaking before cooking makes
the dish lighter.

- CHINESE MIXED VEGETABLES -

8 ounces Chinese green vegetables such as choi
    sum, cut into 1-inch lengths
2 large tomatoes, peeled, seeded and sliced
1 tablespoon brown sugar
1 cup Chinese Vegetable Stock, page 30
1 (3-oz.) can straw mushrooms, drained
1 (3-oz.) can baby corn, drained
1 teaspoon cornstarch
1 teaspoon light soy sauce
1 teaspoon sesame oil

Blanch the greens in boiling water 2 minutes, drain. Sprinkle tomatoes with sugar. In a wok, bring stock to a boil, add tomatoes and simmer 3 minutes, then add the mushrooms and corn. Simmer 6 minutes until the corn is heated through. Lift vegetables from stock and arrange on a warmed serving plate; keep warm. Reserve the cooking stock.

To make sauce, in a small bowl, blend together cornstarch and a little of the reserved stock. In a small saucepan, heat the remaining stock and gradually stir in blended cornstarch. Bring to a boil, stirring, then simmer until thickened. Stir in soy sauce and sesame oil. Pour over vegetables.

Makes 4 servings.

— BRAISED BAMBOO SHOOTS —

1/2 cup cornstarch
1 (15-oz.) can bamboo shoots
2 tablespoons vegetable oil
4 slices gingerroot, peeled
3/4 cup Chinese Vegetable Stock, page 30
1 tablespoon dark soy sauce
1 teaspoon rice wine or dry sherry
1 teaspoon brown sugar
1/2 small red bell pepper, thinly sliced
1/2 small green bell pepper, thinly sliced
1/2 teaspoon sesame oil

Sieve cornstarch onto a plate, toss in bamboo shoot slices to coat lightly and evenly. Shake off excess.

In a wok, heat vegetable oil, add gingerroot, fry 1 minute, then discard. Add bamboo shoots, stir-fry 1 minute, then stir in stock, soy sauce, rice wine or dry sherry and sugar. Simmer 5 minutes until bamboo shoots are just tender. Add bell peppers and cook 3 minutes until softened. Sprinkle with sesame oil.

Makes 4 servings.

— SHANGHAI CASSEROLE —

1/4 cup peanut oil
1-1/2 cups broccoli flowerets
1 (8-oz.) can sliced bamboo shoots, drained
1-1/2 cups thinly sliced carrot
8 dried black winter mushrooms, soaked in hot
    water 25 minutes, drained, liquid reserved
2 (4-oz.) cakes tofu, cut into bite-size pieces
2 teaspoons sea salt
1 teaspoon brown sugar
1 tablespoon dark soy sauce
2 tablespoons rice wine or dry sherry
1 tablespoon Cornstarch Mixture, page 10

In a saucepan, heat oil, add broccoli, bamboo shoots and carrot, and stir-fry 3 minutes. Stir in mushrooms with their soaking liquid and remaining ingredients except Cornstarch Mixture and bring to a boil, stirring.

Reduce heat so liquid simmers, cover and cook 15 minutes. If there is too much liquid, stir in Cornstarch Mixture and heat, stirring until thickened.

Makes 4 servings.

BROCCOLI WITH MUSHROOMS

3 cups water
1/2-inch piece gingerroot, peeled and grated
2 heads broccoli, broken in flowerets
12 dried black winter mushrooms, soaked in hot
　　water 25 minutes, drained
1 teaspoon brown sugar
2 tablespoons peanut oil

Sauce:
1 teaspoon oyster sauce
1 tablespoon light soy sauce
1 tablespoon cornstarch
1 teaspoon sesame oil
1/2 cup Chinese Vegetable Stock, page 30
White pepper

In a saucepan, bring water to a boil; add gingerroot and broccoli and boil 4 minutes. Using a slotted spoon, remove broccoli and keep warm. Add mushrooms and sugar to the water, and cook 6 minutes. Drain well and squeeze out as much liquid as possible; discard stems. Place mushrooms in center of a warmed serving dish and keep warm.

In a wok, heat peanut oil, add broccoli and stir-fry 2 or 3 minutes. Using a slotted spoon, remove, drain on paper towels, then arrange around mushrooms; keep warm.

In a small saucepan, mix together sauce ingredients, bring to a boil, then simmer, stirring constantly 3 minutes. Pour over vegetables.

Makes 4 servings.

— MANDARIN VEGETABLES —

2-1/2 cups Chinese Chicken Stock, page 29
8 ounces snow peas
1 cup carrot, diced
8 ounces fresh lotus root, sliced
4 stalks celery, sliced
1/3 cup peanut oil
4 ounces dried cloud ear mushrooms, soaked in
    hot water 25 minutes, drained
4 ounces dried black winter mushrooms,
    soaked in hot water 25 minutes, drained
1 pound Chinese leaves or spinach, sliced
2 teaspoons cornstarch
1/4 teaspoon brown sugar
1/2 teaspoon salt
4 Potato Nests, opposite, to serve

In a large saucepan, heat stock and bring to a boil, add snow peas, carrot, lotus root and celery and boil 3 minutes. Drain; reserve 1/2 cup stock.

In a wok, heat oil, add mushrooms, then remaining vegetables and stir-fry 5 minutes. In a bowl, stir reserved stock into cornstarch until smooth, then stir into wok with sugar and salt. Bring to a boil, stirring, then simmer until sauce thickens. Serve in Potato Nests.

Makes 4 servings.

POTATO NESTS

1 pound potatoes, finely grated
1 cup cornstarch
2-1/2 cups vegetable oil

Rinse potatoes in several changes of cold water. Drain well and dry on paper towels. Turn into a bowl and stir in cornstarch to mix thoroughly.

Evenly line a 6-inch wire sieve with one-quarter of the potato mixture, then cover with another 6-inch sieve, so the potato is trapped between the two.

In a wok, heat oil until smoking and add the potatoes in the two sieves and deep-fry 2 minutes until crisp and golden. Remove from oil, allow excess to drain off, then carefully remove the sieves. Keep warm. Repeat with the remaining mixture.

Makes 4 servings.

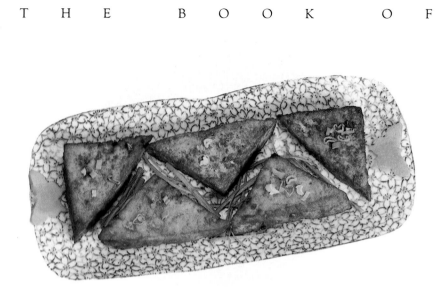

—— DEEP-FRIED BEAN CURD ——

1 tablespoon sea salt
1 tablespoon Chinese five-spice powder
2 tablespoons sugar
1 teaspoon white pepper
1 garlic clove, very finely chopped
4 cakes tofu, halved (1 pound)
2-1/2 cups peanut oil
4 green onions, very finely chopped

In a bowl, mix together salt, five-spice powder, sugar, pepper and garlic. Add one piece of tofu at a time and turn over to evenly coat. Let stand 1 hour.

In a wok, heat oil until smoking, add tofu and deep-fry 5 minutes until puffy and golden. Drain on paper towels and serve immediately sprinkled with the green onion.

Makes 4 servings.

—— SPICED BEAN SPROUTS ——

2 pounds bean sprouts
1-1/2 cups thinly shredded cucumber
4 ounces dried shrimp, soaked in cold water
    25 minutes, drained

Sauce:
1 teaspoon light soy sauce
1 teaspoon sea salt
1/2-inch piece gingerroot, peeled and grated
1 teaspoon ChingKiang vinegar or red wine
    vinegar
2 teaspoons sesame oil
1/2 teaspoon brown sugar

Bring a saucepan of water to a boil. Add bean sprouts, return to a boil and cook 1 minute. Drain, refresh under cold running water, then drain well.

Arrange cucumber around the edge of a plate and put bean sprouts in center. In a bowl, stir together sauce ingredients, then pour over bean sprouts. Sprinkle with dried shrimp.

Makes 4 servings.

VEGETARIAN EIGHT TREASURE

2 tablespoons vegetable oil
4 green onions, sliced
2 garlic cloves, finely chopped
1/2 cup green bell pepper, diced
1/2 cup red bell pepper, diced
2 fresh hot green chiles, seeded and sliced
1 (4-oz.) can water chestnuts, diced
2 (4-oz.) cakes spiced tofu
6 dried black winter mushrooms, soaked in hot
    water 25 minutes, drained
1 cup diced cucumber
2 tablespoons black bean paste
1 teaspoon rice wine or dry sherry
1 teaspoon red bean paste
1 teaspoon dark soy sauce
1 teaspoon brown sugar
1/4 teaspoon ground white pepper
4 ounces deep-fried gluten balls, if desired
    (see Note)
2 tablespoons water
1 teaspoon sesame oil, to serve

In a wok, heat vegetable oil, add green onions and garlic, and stir fry 3 or 4 minutes until just beginning to color. Add bell pepper, chiles and water chestnuts; stir-fry 1 minute. Stir in remaining ingredients except sesame oil and cook 3 minutes.

Serve sprinkled with sesame oil.

Makes 4 servings.

Note: Deep-fried gluten balls are available in packages in Chinese food shops, and specialty delicatessens.

— VEGETARIAN NEW YEAR —

2-1/2 cups vegetable oil
4 cakes tofu, cut into bite-size pieces (1 pound)
6 pieces white ji stick (see Note), if desired
2 ounces dried cloud ear mushrooms, soaked in
    hot water 20 minutes, drained
2 ounces dried black winter mushrooms, soaked
    in hot water 25 minutes, drained
1 (3-oz.) can bamboo shoots, drained and sliced
1 (3-oz.) can water chestnuts, drained and sliced
1/4 cup golden needles, (see Note), soaked in
    warm water 10 minutes, drained
1/3 cup shelled ginko nuts, or blanched
    almonds
1/4 cup water
1 (4-oz.) cake red tofu
1 teaspoon brown sugar
1 tablespoon dark soy sauce

In a wok, heat vegetable oil until smoking,
add tofu and ji sticks, if desired, and fry 3
or 4 minutes until golden and puffy.
Remove and drain on paper towels. Pour
oil from wok leaving just 1/4 cup.
Add mushrooms, bamboo shoots, water
chestnuts and golden needles and stir-fry 5
minutes. Add nuts; stir-fry 1 minute, then
stir in water. Reduce the heat and simmer
4 minutes.

In a bowl, mash together red tofu, sugar
and soy sauce, then stir into wok. Cover
and simmer 10 minutes; if mixture begins
to dry out, add a little more water. Stir
in deep-fried tofu and ji sticks to heat
through.

Makes 4 servings.

Note: Golden needles are dried lilies (they
may also be called tiger lilies), and add a
subtle flavor.
Note: Ji sticks are strips of bean curd.

— MONK'S VEGETABLES —

3 tablespoons vegetable oil
1/2-inch piece gingerroot, peeled and grated
2 garlic cloves, finely chopped
4 ounces bean sprouts
12 gingko nuts or blanched almonds
1-1/2 cups broccoli flowerets
1/2 cup sliced carrots
1 (3-oz.) can bamboo shoots, drained and sliced
12 canned straw mushrooms
12 button mushrooms
10 dried black winter mushrooms, soaked in hot
    water 25 minutes, drained
12 deep-fried gluten balls, if desired, see Note
2 teaspoons rice wine or dry sherry
1 teaspoon brown sugar
1 teaspoon light soy sauce
1/2 cup Chinese Vegetable Stock, page 29
1 teaspoon sesame oil

Sauce:
1 teaspoon cornstarch
1 tablespoon water
1/2 teaspoon dark soy sauce

In a wok, heat 1 tablespoon vegetable oil, add gingerroot and garlic, stir-fry 2 minutes then stir in bean sprouts and stir-fry 1 minute. Remove and keep warm.

Add remaining vegetable oil to wok, heat, then add nuts, broccoli, carrots, bamboo shoots and mushrooms and stir-fry 2 minutes. Add gluten balls if desired, stir 1 minute, then stir in remaining ingredients except sesame oil. Reduce heat and cook 5 minutes.

For the sauce, in a bowl, mix together ingredients, stir into wok and bring to a boil, stirring.   Simmer until thickened. Sprinkle with sesame oil.

Makes 4 servings.

Note: Deep-fried gluten balls are available in packages from Chinese food shops and specialty delicatessens.

SHRIMP PASTE RICE

1-3/4 cups long-grain rice
2 tablespoons shrimp paste
1-inch piece gingerroot, peeled and grated
1 tablespoon peanut oil
1 teaspoon sesame oil
2 green onions, very finely chopped

Cook rice according to package directions until tender but firm to the bite.

Meanwhile, in a bowl, mix together shrimp paste, gingerroot, peanut oil and sesame oil. Transfer rice to a warmed serving bowl and stir in paste mixture. Sprinkle with finely chopped green onions.

Makes 4 servings.

——— GREEN FRIED RICE ———

3/4 cup long-grain rice
3 eggs, beaten
4 tablespoons vegetable oil
8 ounces spring greens or young spinach, ribs
    removed and finely sliced
1 garlic clove, finely chopped
4 green onions, finely chopped
1/2 cup ham, shredded

Cook rice according to package directions
until tender but still firm to the bite. Use
eggs to make a Chinese Omelet (page 24);
cut it into thin strips.

In a wok, heat 1 tablespoon vegetable oil,
add greens or spinach and fry 1 minute;
remove and keep warm. Add remaining oil to the wok, add garlic and green
onions and stir-fry 1 minute, then stir in
the rice. When mixed thoroughly, stir in
ham, greens, omelet slices and salt.

Makes 4 servings.

CRAB FRIED RICE

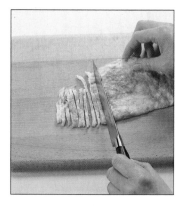

3/4 cup long-grain rice
3 eggs, beaten
1 (3-oz.) can crab meat
2 tablespoons vegetable oil
2-1/3 cups bean sprouts
1 tablespoon light soy sauce
6 green onions, finely chopped
1 teaspoon sesame oil

Cook rice according to package directions until tender but still firm to the bite.

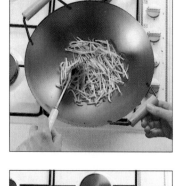

In a bowl, mix together eggs and crab meat with its liquid. Use to make a Chinese Omelet, page 24, then cut it into strips.

In a wok, heat vegetable oil, add bean sprouts and fry 1 minute. Remove from wok and keep warm. Add rice to wok and stir-fry 3 minutes. Stir in soy sauce and cook 2 minutes. Stir in bean sprouts, omelet strips and green onions, and cook 2 or 3 minutes. Serve sprinkled with sesame oil.

Makes 4 servings.

—— VEGETABLE FRIED RICE ——

3/4 long-grain rice
4 tablespoons vegetable oil
2 garlic cloves, finely chopped
1/2-inch piece gingerroot, peeled and grated
1 tablespoon Chinese winter pickle
6 tomatoes, seeded and chopped
1 large red bell pepper, diced
6 dried black winter mushrooms, soaked in hot
    water 25 minutes, drained, squeezed and
    diced
1/3 cup cooked or thawed frozen green peas
1 cup diced cucumber
2 tablespoons light soy sauce

Cook rice according to package directions until tender but still firm to the bite.

In a wok, heat oil, add garlic and ginger-root, fry 30 seconds, then add pickle, tomatoes, bell pepper and mushrooms, peas and cucumber. Stir-fry 4 minutes, then stir in soy sauce. Add rice, mix well and heat through 2 or 3 minutes.

Makes 4 servings.

——— EGG FRIED RICE ———

3/4 cup long-grain rice
3 eggs, beaten
2 tablespoons vegetable oil
1 garlic clove, finely chopped
3 green onions, finely chopped
3/4 cup cooked or thawed frozen green peas
1 tablespoon light soy sauce
1 teaspoon sea salt

Cook rice according to package directions until tender but still firm to the bite.

In a small saucepan, cook eggs over medium-low heat, stirring until lightly scrambled. Remove and keep warm.

In a wok, heat oil, add garlic, green onions and peas and stir-fry 1 minute. Stir in rice to mix thoroughly, then add soy sauce, eggs and salt. Stir to break up egg and mix thoroughly

Makes 4 servings.

──YANG CHOW FRIED RICE──

3/4 cup long-grain rice
3 tablespoons peanut oil
2 medium onions, finely sliced
3 slices gingerroot, peeled and finely chopped
1/2 cup ground pork
1 tablespoon light soy sauce
1 teaspoon brown sugar
2 eggs, beaten
1/2 teaspoon sea salt
Black pepper
3 dried black winter mushrooms, soaked in hot
    water 25 minutes, drained and squeezed
2 large tomatoes, peeled, seeded and chopped
1/3 cup cooked or thawed frozen green peas

Cook rice according to package directions
until tender but still firm to the bite.

In a wok, heat oil, add onions and gingerroot and stir-fry 2 minutes. Stir in pork,
continue stirring 3 minutes until crisp,
then add soy sauce and sugar. Stir-fry 1
minute, then stir in rice. Remove to a
warmed dish and keep warm. Pour eggs
into wok, season with salt and pepper,
then cook stirring 2 or 3 minutes until just
beginning to set. Stir in mushrooms,
tomatoes and peas. Cook 2 or 3 minutes,
then stir in rice mixture.

Makes 4 servings.

PEKING APPLES

1 egg
1/2 cup water
1 cup all-purpose flour
4 crisp eating apples
2-1/2 cups vegetable oil

Syrup:
1 tablespoon vegetable oil
2 tablespoons water
6 tablespoons brown sugar
2 tablespoons corn syrup
Iced water to set

In a large bowl, stir the egg and water into the flour to make a thick batter. Peel, core and thickly slice apples. Dip each apple slice in the batter to evenly coat; allow excess to drain off. In a wok, heat oil until smoking. Add apple pieces in batches and deep-fry 3 minutes until golden brown. Using a slotted spoon, remove to paper towels to drain.

To make syrup, in a small saucepan, gently heat oil, water and sugar, stirring until sugar has dissolved. Simmer 5 minutes, stirring. Stir in corn syrup and boil 5 to 10 minutes until thick and syrupy. Reduce heat to very low. Dip each piece of apple into syrup to coat then place in ice cold water a few seconds. Remove to a serving dish. Repeat with remaining apple. Serve immediately.

Makes 4 servings.

CHINESE FRUIT SOUP

1/2 cup rice wine or dry sherry
Juice and peel of 2 limes
3-1/2 cups water
3-1/2 cups sugar
1 piece lemon grass
4 whole cloves
2-inch cinnamon stick
1 vanilla bean, split
Pinch ground nutmeg
1 teaspoon coriander seeds, lightly crushed
1-1/2 to 2-inch gingerroot piece, peeled and
    thinly sliced
1/4 cup raisins
1 pound prepared fresh fruits, eg. mango,
    strawberries, lychees, star fruit, kiwi fruit.

In a saucepan, place rice wine or dry sherry, lime juice and peel, water, sugar, lemon grass, cloves, cinnamon, vanilla, nutmeg, coriander and gingerroot. Heat gently, stirring until sugar dissolves, then bring to a boil. Reduce heat and simmer 5 minutes. Cool, then strain into a bowl. Add raisins, then chill.

Arrange a selection of prepared fruit in 4 individual serving dishes and spoon syrup over.

Makes 4 servings.

— EXOTIC MANGO MOUSSE —

1 (14-oz) can mandarin orange sections, drained
1 (14-oz) can mango pulp
1-3/4 cups whipping cream
3 tablespoons unflavored gelatin powder
1/3 cup water
4 egg whites
3 tablespoons brown sugar

Reserve a few mandarin sections. In a food processor or blender, process the remaining oranges until smooth, pour into a measuring cup and add water to make 3 cups.

Turn into a large bowl; stir in mango pulp. In another bowl, beat cream until soft peaks form. Fold into mango mixture until just evenly combined. In a small bowl, sprinkle gelatin over water, let soften 5 minutes, then place bowl over a saucepan of boiling water. Stir until gelatin dissolves, then remove bowl from heat and cool slightly. Stir in a little of the mango mixture, then stir into the remaining mango mixture; chill until almost set.

In a clean bowl, beat egg whites until soft peaks form, then beat in sugar. Carefully fold into mango mixture until just evenly mixed. Serve in individual dishes decorated with the reserved mandarin sections.

Makes 8 servings.

Note: Use fresh eggs without cracks.

JASMINE TEA

4 teaspoons jasmine tea
600 ml (20 fl oz/2½ cups) boiling water

Put the tea into a warmed teapot. Pour on the boiling water, stir and leave to infuse about 4 minutes.

Stir again and pour into cups.

Makes 4 servings.

INDEX